A CATHOLIC GUIDE TO MINDFULNESS

Susan Brinkmann, O.C.D.S.

Foreword by Dr. Anthony E. Clark, PhD.

Nihil Obstat: Colin B. Donovan, S.T.L.
　　　　　Censor Librorum

Imprimatur: + Robert J. Baker, S.T.D.
　　　　　　Bishop of Birmingham in Alabama
　　　　　　October 28, 2017, Feast of Saints Simon and Jude

Cover design by Suzanne C. Hurtig
www.SuzanneHurtigDesign.com

Avila Institute for Spiritual Formation
1062 Grand Oaks Drive
Bessemer, AL 35022

Quantity sales. Special discounts are available on quantity purchases by study' groups, parishes, associations, and others. For details, contact the publisher at the address above.

A Catholic Guide to Mindfulness/Susan Brinkmann—1st ed.
ISBN 978-1976532795

Foreword

The Buddhist practice of mindfulness, based upon the Sanskrit word *sati*, is a popular form of meditation to bring a person toward "awakening," or "liberation" from all desire and suffering. Since the 1970s, this eastern religious practice has become a mainstream way of helping relieve anxiety, stress, and depression. Clinical psychologists began prescribing mindfulness, a Buddhist technique for attaining enlightenment, as a common form of treatment, and by the 1980s this eastern mental exercise had become a common "spiritual practice" at Catholic retreat centers. Jesuit, Dominican, Franciscan, and other orders now commonly offer guided retreats on mindfulness with such titles as, "Mindfulness Meditation Retreat: Waking up in Every Moment," and even "Mindfulness for Christmas." This well-researched and well-written book asks the important question: Is the Buddhist technique of mindfulness compatible with Catholicism? And even more importantly, this book asks if mindfulness is an appropriate aid for or replacement of Christian prayer? By the late twentieth century, Dr. Jon Kabat-Zinn, creator of the Stress Reduction Clinic and the Center for Mindfulness in Medicine, mixed together what he had learned from the Zen Master, Thich Nhat Hanh, with what he had studied of human psychology to create mindfulness, now offered as "medical" treatment at most health clinics and hospitals.

Several factors have contributed to the popularity of mindfulness among practicing Catholics, including a wave of Catholic interest in eastern spirituality following the wake of the writings by Father Thomas Merton, a Trappist monk from the Abbey of Gethsemani in Kentucky. After reading the Zen writings of D. T. Suzuki, Merton wrote his famous reflection of Buddhist spirituality, *Zen and the Birds of Appetite*. He later traveled to Asia, where he kept a detailed journal, wherein he wrote such remarks as, "Our real journey in life is interior: it is a matter of growth, deepening, and of an ever greater surrender to the creative action of love and grace in our hearts. Never was it more necessary for us to respond to that action."[1] For many Catholics, Merton's admiration for Buddhist and Daoist thought, along with his appeal for the interior life, led them to view eastern spiritual practices as a way to deepen — perhaps even fulfill — the spiritual void they sensed in their own prayer life. Whether or not Merton intended his writings to inspire the mixing of Christian prayer and Buddhist meditation, many who followed after him published works that did just that.

The Jesuit priest and psychotherapist, Father Anthony de Mello, who many view as following in the footsteps of Merton, published his influential *Sadhana — A way to God*, in 1978, which describes what he envisioned as Christian exercises in eastern form. De Mello's popular fusion of Christianity and eastern religious practice so concerned the prefect of the Congregation of the Doctrine of the Faith, Cardinal Joseph Ratzinger, that he wrote a warning against such ideas. Ratzinger wrote

---

[1] Thomas Merton, *The Asian Journal of Thomas Merton* (New York: New Directions, 1975), 296.

that in de Mello's books, "one notices a progressive distancing from the essential contents of the Christian faith," and that, "in place of the revelation which has come in the person of Jesus Christ, he substitutes an intuition of God without form or image, to the point of speaking of God as a pure void."[2] Some have asserted that this same critique of incorporating such eastern ideas and practices into the spiritual life of Catholics applies equally to the meditation techniques of mindfulness.

Another important issue this book faces is the important distinction between so-called scientific psychology and spiritual realities. Practitioners of mindfulness often assert that it is a non-religious and scientifically proven remedy for mental health challenges. Firstly, this book clearly engages the claim that mindfulness is non-religious; its founder, Kabat-Zinn, admits as much. And secondly, this book reveals that the distinction between the "science" of psychology and the spiritual properties of human thought is not as easily determined as persons such as Jon Kabat-Zinn insist. In truth, the field of psychology and the supernatural realities known to Christians are often at odds, and this point is clearly made in the introduction to the first volume of the eastern Christian spiritual classic, *The Philokalia*:

> Something similar applies with respect to the whole psychological understanding which these texts both presuppose and elucidate. In effect, one is confronted with a psychology, or science of the soul, many of whose fundamental features — particularly perhaps in relation to the role of the demons — are completely unrecognized

---

[2] Joseph Cardinal Ratzinger, "Concerning the Writings of Father Anthony de Mello, SJ," 24 June 1998.

by, not to say at odds with, the theories of most modern psychologists.[3]

This is to say that what one person calls "science," or what another calls "non-religious," is actually very much related to the spiritual and religious realm. How one "meditates" or prays profoundly affects the present state and future condition of her or his soul. As this introduction suggests, Christians and clinical psychologists do not always agree on the very nature of "psychology."

Common sense tells us that the direction one drives a car determines the place one arrives at, and spiritual practice is no different. When one understands well the intentions of Christian prayer and mindfulness, it is clear that, at their root, they point in contrasting directions. Buddhist techniques aim entirely *at the locus of human experience*, while Christian prayer is directed *through and well beyond the human experience* toward God. The fifth century Theravada monk, Buddhaghosa, is one of the most influential Buddhist writers on the intention and meaning of meditation practices such as *sati*, or mindfulness. Mindfulness, he suggests, is intended to remove one from the external world; it is largely anti-relational, for relationships bring about attachment, and attachment causes suffering. Buddhaghosa writes that:

> Relatives are no more closely united than travelers who
> for a while meet at an inn, and then part again, losing
> sight of each other. This world is by nature split up into
> disjointed parts; no one really belongs to anyone else; it is
> held together by cause and effect, as loose sand by a

---

[3] *The Philokalia*, Vol. 1., trans. by G. E. Palmer, Philip Sherrard, and Kallistos Ware (London: Faber and Faber, 1979), 16-17.

clenched fist. . ... We see relatives behave unkindly, while non-relatives may show us kindness.[4]

Certainly, a relative or friend is capable of being unkind, and it is wise to avoid the abuse of others, but the goal of Buddhist meditation, according to Buddhaghosa, is to become entirely self-focused and free from the joys and attachments of relationships so that one can escape from pain and the misery of reincarnation. Christianity views relationships not as problematic, but as a requirement of how we grow in charity and love. St. Paul writes, "And let us consider how to stir up one another to love and good works, not neglecting to meet together, as is the habit of some, but encouraging one another, and all the more as you see the Day drawing near."[5]

Unlike the Christian call to relationship with God and others regardless of personal cost, Buddhaghosa suggests that, "One who delights in solitude is content with his own company," and he recommends that to meditate one should "shun familiarity with others, as if they were a thorn in the flesh."[6]

And finally, this book does more than explore the differences between Christian spirituality and mindfulness; it also provides examples of Catholic methods of prayer that are deeply freeing for Christians, and also effective toward attaining authentic serenity and insight. The teachings of St. Teresa of Avila are thus discussed in the concluding chapter. In contrast to the advice of Buddhaghosa, St. Teresa wrote that:

---

[4] Buddhaghosa, "The Progressive Steps of Meditation," in *Buddhist Scriptures,* trans. by Edward Conze (London: Penguin Books, 1959), 110-111.
[5] Hebrews 10:24-25.
[6] Buddhaghosa, "The Progressive Steps of Meditation," 107-108.

> Mental prayer in my opinion is nothing else than an intimate sharing between friends; it means taking time frequently to be alone with Him who we know loves us. The important thing is not to think much but to love much and so do that which best stirs you to love. Love is not great delight but desire to please God in everything.[7]

Not only does she describe prayer as a relational activity, but it is also directed toward God, who is strikingly absent in the aims or beliefs of Buddhism and its practice of mindfulness. As one reads in this book, Christians are not alone, and to turn entirely self-ward as proposed by a pure exercise of mindfulness is tantamount to creating a distance between oneself and her or his creator. In his final moments, the Buddha said to his disciples: "Behold, O monks, this is my last advice to you. All component things in the world are impermanent. They are not lasting. Work hard to gain your own salvation."[8] Mindfulness practice, like this final exhortation, informs the practitioner to concentrate within, aware only of the present moment, and heal the self, to gain her or his *own* salvation. Christians understand that such a practice proposes a contrary path to "salvation" as revealed in and through Jesus Christ who admonished us to embrace suffering on the path to salvation by taking up the cross and following Him. For we are told in Sacred Scripture, "Have I not commanded you? Be strong and courageous. Do not be afraid; do not be discouraged, for the Lord your God will be with you wherever you go."[9]

---

[7] Quoted in Kathleen Beckman, *When Women Pray* (Manchester, NH: Sophia Institute Press, 2017), 34.

[8] The Buddha, *Maha-Parivirvana Sutra*, Part 6: 8.

[9] Joshua 1:9.

This timely book provides answers to the many Catholics who have asked priests, sisters, and scholars whether such practices as mindfulness are appropriate or helpful to Christian spiritual growth and personal peace. The author Susan Brinkman has not written this book to create antagonisms between Catholics and Buddhists or those who practice mindfulness, but rather to objectively explore the truth claims of both and reveal whether or not they are compatible, particularly with respect to the growing fad and focus on mindfulness. To assert that Catholics and Buddhists hold equal claims to the truth, and that their spiritual practices may be interchanged without discrimination, is to ignore the very nature of truth and Christian revelation. While Catholics and Buddhists may share many important values, such as compassion and the quest for spiritual advancement, a religion that believes in and seeks to commune with God will always view reality through a different lens than those that do not. Joseph Ratzinger has written that, "When the existence of God is denied, freedom is not enhanced, but deprived of its basis and thus distorted."[10] Freedom, Ratzinger continues, is inextricably bound to truth, and the truth held by Christian revelation has inspired Catholics through the millennia to approach prayer and meditation in ways entirely unlike what one encounters in clinical, or religious, mindfulness. This helpful guide confronts these issues with charity and truth; it is not interested in spiteful religious polemics, but rather in providing precise answers to pressing questions in the minds of a rising number of concerned Catholics.

St. John of the Cross has perhaps described best what all prayer and meditation must seek to do. "Contemplation is nothing else but a secret,

---

[10] Joseph Ratzinger, *Truth and Tolerance: Christian Belief and World Religions*, trans. by Henry Taylor (San Francisco: Ignatius Press, 2003), 258.

peaceful, and loving infusion of God," he writes, "which if admitted, will set the soul on fire with the spirit of love."[11]

Anthony E. Clark, Ph.D.
Edward B. Lindaman Endowed Chair
Whitworth University

---

[11] St. John of the Cross, *The Dark Night of the Soul*, trans. by David Lewis (London: Thomas Baker, 1908), 45.

Contents

Foreword i

Ch. 1: What is Mindfulness? 1

Ch. 2: Mindfulness Goes Mainstream 17

Ch. 3: The Science of Mindfulness 33

Ch. 4: Do Buddhism and Catholicism Mix? 51

Ch. 5: Mindfulness and Christian Prayer 67

Ch. 6: Christian Alternatives to Mindfulness 87

About the Author 109

Chapter One

What is Mindfulness?

It was not very long ago when the term "mindful" was used to describe a state of attention that parents expected of their children. Today, it's a buzzword for the latest eastern-style meditation and mental discipline technique heralded as effective for everything from gaining self-awareness and inner calm to treating Post Traumatic Stress (PTSD) and other anxiety disorders. Mindfulness practitioners, once found only among Buddhists, can now be found among the ranks of corporate executives, medical doctors, teachers, secretaries, Hollywood stars, sports enthusiasts and even clergy. So what do people find so fascinating about this practice?

To answer that question, let's start out with a basic definition. "[M]indfulness is what arises when you pay attention, on purpose, in the present moment, non-judgmentally, and as if your life depended on it."[12]

It is a "state of active, open attention on the present" by which you observe your thoughts and feelings as if from a distance, without judging

---

[12]Kabat-Zinn, Jon, *Mindfulness for Beginners* (Boulder, Colorado: *Sounds True*, 2012) pg. 17

them to be good or bad. "Instead of letting your life pass you by, mindfulness means living in the moment and awakening to experience."[13]

Although mindfulness is primarily a meditation technique, it can also be practiced as simply disciplining yourself to pay attention to where you are, what you're doing, and how you're feeling at any given moment. You're not to judge anything, such as why you are where you are, or why you're doing what you're doing, or if you should be doing something else, or if your feelings are good or bad at the moment. You are simply making yourself aware of what *is*.

For example, if you're drinking a cup of tea, you take note of how it tastes, the feel of the cup against your lips, the scent of the tea, the warmth of the liquid as it enters your mouth and courses down your throat, the thoughts that cross your mind as you swallow, etc. If you begin to think that perhaps the tea should be a bit sweeter or the noise of a truck on the road outside is a bit too loud, you simply return your thoughts to what *is* — a sip of tea that is a tad too bitter and a noisy truck passing by. This practice is supposed to help stop us from "living in our minds" so to speak, worrying about what might happen if we do this or that, how things could be so much better if only this or that would happen, why this person said what she did and that person didn't do what was expected. Mindfulness helps us to jump off that revolving Ferris-wheel of "what if" and allows us to deal only with "what is."

This is why the purpose of becoming more mindful is to learn how "to inhabit another domain of mind that we are, as a rule, fairly out of

---

[13] *Psychology Today*, accessed online at https://www.psychologytoday.com/basics/mindfulness

touch with. And that is what you might call the being mode of mind."[14] Our multi-tasking lifestyles have left us too busy and scattered and inattentive. We have become more a *human doing* than a *human being*, the experts say, and thereby forget *who* is doing all the doing and why. "Mindfulness reminds us that it is possible to shift from a doing mode to a being mode through the application of attention and awareness. Then our doing can come out of our being and be much more integrated and effective."[15]

How is it practiced?

For those who want to practice mindfulness on a minimal level, there are a variety of ways to do so, from engaging in "mindful mini-breaks" at the office which consist of taking a moment to just be where you are. Or it can be to engage in walking or eating or tooth-brushing "meditations" that call for you to take a moment to just be mindful of exactly where you are and what you're doing. This is not too different from the old-fashioned "take a deep breath" or a "step back" or a "count to 10" moment.

But for the most part, the mindfulness trend we're experiencing today is much more involved than this and usually calls for some kind of meditation exercise.

Body Scan Meditation

This is by far one of the most popular forms of mindful meditation and the technique most often taught by health care professionals. The

---

[14] Mindfulness for Beginners, pg. 17
[15] Ibid, pg. 18

purpose of the body scan is "to bring awareness to each part of our body sequentially, to see how it is today — not to check in to change or judge the body, which we're apt to do, but just to experience it and see what's there."[16]

Before beginning, the practitioner states one's intention for the meditation and agrees to let go of the past and future and not to be judgmental about anything one feels in one's body. The practitioner then lays down and takes notice of all parts of the body, in a systematic way, from the balls of the feet to the top of the head. One by one, the practitioner works through each part of the body, focusing on whatever sensations one might be feeling in one's toes, ankles, calves, shins, knees, etc. This can be used as an opportunity to identify areas of tension such as can be found in the jaw, neck, shoulders, etc.

Once a part of the body is scanned, one allows awareness of that part to fade away as one moves to the next area. This is done throughout the body, including the head. After scanning the head, the practitioner connects the entire body together, such as feeling the connection of the head to the neck, of the neck to the torso, etc. The final step is to feel the skin around the whole body.

Movement Meditation

This form of meditation typically involves some type of yoga, qi gong, or other type of mind-body exercise. Practitioners begin by focusing on their breathing, followed by bodily sensations as they perform the movements. This practice also involves letting go of whatever thoughts or emotions arise during the session.

---

[16]Valentine, Vicki, "A Crash Course in Body Scan Meditation", *NPR*, February 28, 2007.

Vietnamese Buddhist monk, author and teacher, Thich Nhat Hanh, has developed a series of Mindful Movements which are described as being "simple, deep motions, based in yoga and tai-chi."[17] They are simple moves such as arm circles, reaching toward the sky, opening the arms to the side, squatting "like a frog," touching the ground, etc., all of which are performed slowly and mindfully.

For example, in the "Open Like a Flower" movement, the practitioner breathes in, lifts the arms to the side with the palms up until their arms are horizontal to the ground. Breathing out, they are instructed to touch the shoulders with the fingertips. Breathing in, the arms are again extended and, breathing out, the fingers are brought back to touch the shoulder. "When you breathe in, you are like a flower opening to the warm sun. Breathing out, the flower closes."[18]

Breathing Space Meditation

This is described as a short three-minute exercise that begins with sitting down and focusing attention on the sensation of sitting, of the feel of the feet on the floor, the position of the spine, neck, and head. Either close the eyes or fix them on a spot about five feet in front and hold the spot in a steady gaze. When ready, the practitioner looks into the mind and asks himself, "What is my experience right now? What thoughts are present to me? What am I feeling?" The practitioner is advised to observe these thoughts and feelings without any need to alter them.

In the second stage of this short meditation, the practitioner

---

[17] Thich Nhat Hanh and Wietske Vriezen, *Mindful Movements: 10 Exercises for Well-Being* (Berkley, California: *Parallax Press*, 2008)
[18] Ibid

attempts to let go of the contents of the mind and brings their attention to a single point of focus on the breath, such as where it is coursing in and out of the nostrils or in the rising and falling of the chest, thus giving the mind only one thing to do.

The last stage is to expand awareness to the body as a whole, from the crown of the head to the souls of the feet, and into the room and the space around themselves.[19]

Expanding Awareness Meditation

Commonly referred to as sitting meditation, it is similar to the breathing space meditation in its practice but is not limited to just three minutes of focus on a single point. Instead, it is meant to develop into an open awareness of whatever is most predominant in the person's consciousness. The point is to not to engage it, but just to observe it. If the practitioner finds himself being pulled into this stream of thought, he simply returns to the state of just observing it and uses his breathing and bodily sensations as a kind of anchor to bring him back to the present.

"The thoughts can take any form, they can have any content and they can be either neutral or very highly charged. If thoughts come up that have fear in them, then just be aware of fear being here and letting these thoughts come and go. The same for worries, preoccupations, and so on. Regardless of the feeling that a thought might create for you, just observe it as simply a thought and let it be here without pursuing it or without rejecting it. Noticing that from moment to moment, new

---

[19] Segal, Zindel, "The Three-Minute Breathing Space Practice", Mindful.org, June 8, 2016

thoughts will come and go."[20]

People are advised to practice this type of meditation anywhere from ten to thirty minutes with the goal of eventually extending it to forty minutes or an hour.[21]

These are the most common forms of mindfulness practice which generally fall into three degrees of intensity.

The lowest degree of intensity involves simple practices of awareness or short meditation exercises such as those offered through self-help books, downloadable recordings, YouTube videos, etc. Popular apps, such as Headspace, which was developed by an experienced mindfulness teacher, also fall into this category.

Moderate intensity practices are those most commonly used in therapy and involve daily practice of up to forty minutes in duration with patients being mindful of both pleasant and unpleasant feelings and/or memories and learning how to work skillfully with these experiences.

The most intensive way to practice mindfulness would be in a retreat setting where the participant meditates for many hours each day, often for a week or more.

In this type of meditation, the participant aims to achieve a state of powerful concentration in order achieve awakening. This is done by progressing through a set of meditative attainments referred to as jhanas, or "absorptions" which are states of "deep mental unification which result from the centering of the mind upon a single object with

---

[20]"Meditation Scripts, Guided Sitting Meditation", *Mindfulness Hamilton* blog, November 5, 2013

[21]Wegala, Karen Kissel, "How to Practice Mindful Meditation," *Psychology Today*, January 19, 2010

such power of attention that a total immersion in the object takes place."[22]

For example, the first jhana is described as a "meditative state of profound concentration and stillness in which the mind becomes fully immersed and literally absorbed in the chosen object of attention. . . .. If the breath — a popular choice because it is what the Buddha had taken up when he became enlightened — is chosen, one focuses completely just under the nose. One is aware of the breath coming in and out. And one remains undistracted, unagitated, and wakeful. Eventually, one will see the breath. It appears as a tuft of cotton, a glow, or a bright moon released from clouds. Yet, one keeps applying attention only to the spot under the nose not turning attention to anything else. One is 'mindful' just of the breath in that area outside the nose. By ignoring the light, the light will approach where attention is being paid. In time, it will become the breath. . . .."

Eventually, as one continues to practice this meditation on a daily basis, "when the light is steady, brilliant, and one is able to control it making it bigger or smaller by simply determining that it be so, one is ready to 'absorb.' One literally does so by forming the intention and making the determination to merge. One becomes one with the light."[23]

Thus far, we obtained an overview of mindfulness and its practice, but in order to deepen our understanding, we must now consider its origins.

---

[22] Gunaratna, Henepola, "The Jhanas in Theravada Buddhist Meditation," 1995, accessed at accesstoinsight.org.

[23] "Meditation Absorption: The First Jhana," *Wisdom Quarterly, American Buddhist Journal*, April 28, 2010

The Origins of Mindfulness

Mindfulness, as it is practiced today in the West, is referred to as "secularized," yet even the pioneers of this secularization don't hesitate to honor its Buddhist roots.

"[I]t is fair to say that, historically speaking, the most refined and developed articulations of mindfulness and how to cultivate it stem from the Buddhist tradition, and Buddhist texts and teachings constitute an invaluable resource for deepening our understanding and appreciation of mindfulness and the subtleties of its cultivation," says Jon Kabat-Zinn, one of the pioneers of western mindfulness.[24]

Mindfulness, which is the English translation of the Pali term *sati*, is referred to in Buddhism as Right Concentration or Right Mindedness and is the seventh step in the Noble Eightfold Path, which is the fourth of the Four Noble Truths taught by the Buddha.

The Buddha was a Hindu man named Siddhartha Gautama who lived in India around 500-400 B.C. Siddhartha had a series of four visions in which he saw an old man, a sick man, a corpse, and a wandering holy man, from which he deduced that life involves aging, sickness, and death. He understood the fourth vision, that of the wandering holy man, to mean that he was to leave his family and seek religious enlightenment in order to be freed from this cycle of suffering.

"For six years, Siddhartha wandered as a monk, practicing many forms of asceticism. However, since none of these practices led to enlightenment, he abandoned them. Legend says that one day he decided

---

[24] Kabat-Zinn, Jon, *Mindfulness for Beginners*, (Boulder, Colorado: *Sounds True*, 2012) pg. 22

to meditate under a 'bo' tree, vowing not to leave until he gained enlightenment. After many hours of Hindu meditation, enlightenment came. From then on, he was called Buddha which means 'enlightened one' and his insights became known as the Four Noble Truths."[25]

The Four Noble Truths[26] are:

1) *Life is suffering*. Referred to as Dukkha, its literal meaning is "that which is difficult to bear" and refers to suffering, stress, pain, anguish, affliction and dissatisfaction.

2) *The cause of suffering is desire*. This "desire" is defined as grasping, clinging, or aversion. It is trying to control things either by grabbing hold of them or by pushing away.

3) *To be free from suffering we must detach from desire*. If we detach from suffering, we achieve what is known as Nirvana, or the state of being free from grasping and controlling. It is known as supreme Bodhi or awakening to the true nature of reality and to our own true nature.

4) *Following the Eightfold Path leads to Awakening.* This path is a process designed to help a person move beyond the conditioned responses that obscure one's true nature.

This fourth truth presents a kind of blueprint for conquering desire. It consists of eight practices to be undertaken:

1) **Samma[27]-Ditthi,** or Right View, which means acquiring

---

[25] Benkovic, Johnnette, *The New Age Counterfeit* (Goleta, California: *Queenship*, 1993) pg. 14

[26] Allan, John, "The Eight-Fold Path", Buddhist Studies, Buddha Dharma Education Association and Buddhanet

[27] Samma means "summit" in English

knowledge of the truth.

2) **Samma-Sankappa**, or Right Intention, which refers to forming the intention to resist evil by acquiring right thought and attitude, thus enabling a person to act from love and compassion.

3) **Samma-Vaca**, or Right Speech, means to say nothing to hurt others and to be clear, truthful, uplifting and non-harmful in our communication.

4) **Samma-Kammanta**, or Right Action, means respecting life, morality, and property, it is the acquisition of an ethical foundation for life based on the principle of non-exploitation of oneself and others.

5) **Samma-Ajiva**, or Right Livelihood, means acquiring a proper livelihood by being ethically employed in an occupation that does not harm or exploit others.

6) **Samma-Vayama**, or Right Effort, consists of striving to rid one's mind of evil by maintaining a positive attitude and rejecting thoughts of jealousy, anger, etc.

7) **Samma-Sati**, or Right Mindfulness, means controlling thoughts by maintaining awareness and focus on the present moment.

8) **Samma-Samadhi**, or Right Concentration, refers to Samadhi, which is the establishment and absorption of the mind and being in a single point of consciousness and awareness. This refers to the state of enlightenment sometimes called Buddahood.

In Buddhism, the ultimate goal is not merely to eradicate desire, which is the cause of suffering, but to become enlightened and thus to be freed from the suffering that results from ignorance. However, the Buddhist does not believe this is possible as long as the person is "en-self-ed", meaning he still believes in the existence of the self.

This is because in Buddhism, "The central core of every being is not an unchanging soul but a life-current, an ever-changing stream of energy which is never the same for two consecutive seconds. The self, considered as an eternal soul, therefore, is a delusion, and when regarded from the ultimate standpoint it has no reality; and it is only within this delusion of selfhood that ultimate suffering can exist."[28]

In other words, in order to achieve enlightenment, which is to be liberated from all suffering and thus freed from the results of karma and the cycle of reincarnation, one must achieve self-extinction.

The way to this enlightenment or nirvana (which means "blowing out") is not a scholarly study, but is instead based upon the practice of meditation and mindfulness. For the Buddhist, mindfulness is not intended to decrease stress "but to foster insights into subtle concepts (or facts from the Buddhist worldview), including impermanence and emptiness."[29]It was the way of the Buddha himself, as he describes in the *Samyutta Nikaya*:

> Concentration by mindfulness of breathing, when
>
> developed and cultivated, is of great fruit and benefit . . ..

---

[28]Bullen, Leonard, "Buddhism: A Method of Mind Training," *Access to Insight (Legacy Edition)*, 5 June 2010, http://www.accesstoinsight.org/lib/authors/bullen/bl042.html

[29]Murray, Greg, "Do I have a self? (and other useful questions from Buddhist mindfulness)", Australian and New Zealand Journal of Psychiatry, June 22, 2015

> I too, monks, before my enlightenment, while I was still a
> bodhisatta, not yet fully enlightened, generally dwelt in
> this dwelling. While I generally dwelt in this dwelling,
> neither my body nor my eyes became fatigued and my
> mind, by not clinging, was liberated from the taints.
> Therefore, monks, if a monk wishes: 'May neither my
> body nor my eyes become fatigued and may my mind, by
> not clinging, be liberated from the taints,' this same
> concentration by mindfulness of breathing should be
> closely attended to.[30]

This was the Buddha's belief not only before enlightenment, but afterward as well.

According to Theravadan Buddhist Justin Merritt, a teacher at the Northfield Buddhist Meditation Center in Minnesota, the same text quoted above reveals that mindfulness of body (breathing) continued to be the mainstay of the Buddha's practice. Merritt tells the story of the Buddha, after his enlightenment, who was about to enter into a three-month Vassa — known as a rains retreat — which he wanted to spend in total isolation. He told his monks that he didn't want to see anyone except those who were bringing him food. What did he do for those three months?

"If followers of other teachers ask how I spent my rains retreat, just tell them he mostly spent his rains retreat in the concentration that comes from mindfulness of breathing."[31]

---

[30] *Samyutta Nikaya,* Vol. II, 54.1.8 translation by Bhikkhu Bodhi
[31] *Samyutta Nikaya,* Vol. II, 54.2.1, quoted in "How did the Buddha meditate?", Simple Suttas, a Blog of Original Buddhism

This makes sense because in Buddhism, the mind is everything.

"It is a significant fact, and worth pondering upon, that the Bible commences with the words, 'In the beginning God created the heaven and the earth . . .' while the *Dhammapada*, one of the most beautiful and popular books of the Buddhist Scriptures, opens with the words, 'Mind precedes things, dominates them, creates them (translation by Bhikku Kassapa). These momentous words are the quiet and uncontending but unshakable reply of the Buddha to that biblical belief. Here the roads of these two religions part . . .. Mind is the fount of all the good and evil that arises within and befalls us from without."[32]

As the Buddha himself once said, "Whatsoever there is of evil, connected with evil, belonging to evil — all issues from mind. Whatever there is of good, connected with good, belonging to good — all issues from mind."

Many Buddhists believe that mindfulness can help us to better understand that whatever exists in our mind is created by us; therefore, there can never be a God-Creator, only a self-creator.

Mindfulness, then, is essential to the practice of Buddhism and explains why it holds such an important place in the framework of Buddhist doctrine. It recurs frequently, and in many contexts, in Buddhist scriptures, and is a member of several groups of doctrinal terms.

For example, in addition to the term "Right Mindfulness" which is the seventh factor in the Noble Eightfold Path, mindfulness is also the first of the seven so-called Factors of Enlightenment because it is considered basic for the full development of the other six factors.

---

[32]Nyanaponika, Thera, The Heart of Buddhist Meditation: Satipatthna: A Handbook of Mental Training, (Samuel Weiser: 1973) pg. 21

Mindfulness is also one of the Five Faculties — mindfulness, confidence, energy, concentration, and wisdom. "Mindfulness, apart from being a basic faculty in its own right, has the important function of watching over the even development and balance of the other four . . ."[33]

The key text on mindfulness in the Buddhist canon is the *Satipatthana Sutta*, which translates in English to mean *the Scripture of the Foundations of Mindfulness*. This text offers the fullest explanation of the practice that has been in use for centuries, up to the present time.

In the *Satipatthana Sutta* there are four sections which are known as the Four Foundations of Mindfulness. The first of these sections is mindfulness of the body. The second is mindfulness of feelings. The third section is mindfulness of the mind or consciousness. The fourth section is mindfulness of mental objects.

Much of what is currently presented as mindfulness practice is derived from the first of these sections; however, these sections are meant to be viewed as a progression with each step serving as a foundation for the next. This means that mindfulness, as it is practiced today, is, and always has been, foundational to the practice of Buddhism.

Even though there are different schools of Buddhism, such as the Theraveda, the Mahayana and Mantrayana, and different types of meditation such as vipassana and samatha, "Mindfulness, as the faculty of sustaining continuous attention on a chosen object, is indispensable for all kinds of meditation."[34]

So how did this ancient practice become so popular in the contemporary world? This will be the focus of our next chapter.

---

[33] Ibid, pg. 29

[34] Wallace, B. Alan, "A Mindful Balance," Santa Barbara Institute for Consciousness Studies, accessed online at www.sbinstitute.com

Chapter Two

Mindfulness Goes Mainstream

As we have just learned, mindfulness is an ancient practice that for centuries was found largely in Buddhist temples throughout the East, but this all began to change in the early 1960's during the turbulent era of the Vietnam War and the radical peace activism it spawned.

It was during this time that a Vietnamese Buddhist monk named Thich Nhất Hanh, sometimes called the "Father of Mindfulness," made his first visit to the United States.

The year was 1961 and Vietnam was already in the grips of violent upheaval. America was actively involved in training the army of South Vietnamese President Ngo Dinh Diem and anyone suspected of being in line with the Viet Minh, a national front organization aligned with the president of North Vietnam, Ho Chi Minh, was arrested and thrown into prison. By 1957, the Viet Minh had already started to spill blood in South Vietnam in a new campaign of guerrilla warfare, while the National Liberation Front, known as the Vietcong, were forming in Hanoi.

This was the world in which the gentle Nhất Hanh was forced to live. At the time, he had only been an ordained monk for eleven years but had already distinguished himself in the movement to renew Vietnamese Buddhism. As a young bhikshu (monk), he was the first to study a secular subject at a university in Saigon and to ride a bicycle. Having studied under a forty-first generation (Rinzai) Master of the Lieu Quan School of Vietnamese Buddhism, he was amply qualified to co-found a temple in Saigon just a year after ordination, and then to be appointed editor-in-chief of *Vietnamese Buddhism*, the periodical of the All Vietnam Buddhist Association just six years later.[35]

But life was not normal in Vietnam and it was a reality everyone had to be face.

"When war came to Vietnam, monks and nuns were confronted with the question of whether to adhere to the contemplative life and stay meditating in the monasteries, or to help those around them suffering under the bombings and turmoil of war. Thich Nhất Hanh was one of those who chose to do both, and in doing so founded the Engaged Buddhism movement."[36]

Engaged Buddhists were those who sought to apply insights from their meditation practice and studies to situations of social, political, environmental, and economic suffering.

In 1961, in the midst of this national turmoil, Nhất Hạnh traveled to the United States to teach Comparative Religion at Princeton University. A year later, he went to Columbia University in New York where he taught and researched Buddhism. He returned to his native

---

[35]"Thich Nhat Hanh," BBC, Retrieved 04/10/17

[36]"The Miracle of Mindfulness", Thich Nhat Hanh USA Tour 2015, accessed at website https://tnhtour.org/thich-nhat-hanh/

Vietnam in 1963 in order to devote himself to the aid of his fellow monks and to promoting non-violent peace efforts. While there, he founded the Van Hanh Buddhist University in Saigon, the *La Boi Publishing House*, and an activist peace magazine.

According to the Order of Interbeing,[37] a new order he established in 1966 that is based on the traditional Buddhist Bodhisattva precepts, he was eventually exiled from Vietnam and not permitted to return until years later. As the head of this monastic and lay group, he began to promulgate his teachings on the moral imperatives known as the Five Mindfulness Trainings and the Fourteen Precepts.

The hallmark of Thich Nhất Hanh's teaching of mindfulness was its basis on conscious breathing and of being fully aware of the present moment — just like the Buddha. He taught that the only way to truly develop peace in oneself and the world is by living in the present moment through the practice of mindfulness.

In 1966, Nhất Hanh returned to the U.S. to lead a symposium in Vietnamese Buddhism at Cornell University. While in the States, he stopped by Gethsemani Abbey where he met with Thomas Merton. Not long after this meeting, when Vietnam threatened to block Nhất Hạnh's re-entry to the country, Merton published an essay of solidarity entitled, "Nhất Hanh is my Brother."[38]

"I have said Nhất Hanh is my brother, and it is true," Merton writes. "We are both monks, and we have lived the monastic life about the same

---

[37]"Thich Nhat Hanh," Order of Interbeing, accessed Internet Archives https://web.archive.org/web/20080102023137/http://www.interbeing.org.u k/teachers/thay.htmlat

[38]Merton: Collected Essays, excerpt reprinted at Buddhistdoor Global, May 1, 2011.

number of years. We are both poets, both existentialists. I have far more in common with Nhất Hanh than I have with many Americans, and I do not hesitate to say it."

He goes on to praise Nhất Hanh as being a free man, moved by the spiritual dynamic of a tradition of religious compassion who bears witness to the "spirit of Zen."

After being exiled from his homeland, Nhất Hanh settled in France where he founded a community, known as the Sweet Potato Community, which now resides at Plum Village near Bordeaux in southwest France. The first monastic community founded by Nhất Hanh in the West, it has since grown into Europe's largest Buddhist monastery with over 200 resident monks and nuns who are living and practicing the art of "living in harmony with one another and with the Earth."

"At Plum Village we weave mindfulness into all our daily activities, training ourselves to be mindful throughout the day: while eating, walking, working, or enjoying a cup of tea together. Plum Village is a home away from home, and a beautiful, nourishing, simple environment in which to cultivate the mind of awakening."[39]

Since 1983, Nhất Hanh has been traveling around the world offering lectures and mindfulness retreats, particularly in Europe and the United States. He has published over 100 titles on mindfulness and meditation, as well as on Engaged Buddhism. He has sold over three million books in the U.S. alone, such as *The Miracle of Mindfulness, Being Peace, The Art of Power,* and *True Love.* For this reason, he is considered to be a pioneer in bringing Buddhism to the West where he founded six monasteries

---

[39] Accessed at https://plumvillage.org/about/plum-village/

and dozens of practice centers in America and Europe as well as over 1,000 local mindfulness practice communities known as "sanghas."[40] [41]

Nhất Hanh, who recently suffered a stroke, influenced thousands of people from all walks of life. One of those people was a young biomedical scientist named Jon Kabat-Zinn who would one day develop the Mindfulness-Based Stress Reduction (MBSR) program at what is now the Center for Mindfulness in Medicine, Health Care and Society at the University of Massachusetts Medical School.

Between the years of 1964-1971, while Kabat-Zinn was training in molecular biology at MIT in the laboratory of Nobel Laureate Salvador Luria. A popular Zen missionary named Philip Kapleau came to speak at the university. Kabat-Zinn was in the audience that day and was inspired by what he heard. He began a daily meditation practice as well as the study of meditation at the Insight Meditation Society where he would one day teach. At the time, he was pondering his "karmic assignment" and wondering where his place in life was to be.

After marrying his wife, Myla, and starting a family, he became a faculty member in the Biology Department at Brandeis University, where he taught molecular genetics and a science for non-science majors which he described as "an opportunity for teaching meditation and yoga as pathways to a first-person experience of biology." He briefly served as Director of the Cambridge Zen Center under the Korean Zen Master, Seung Sahn, where he was also his student and a Dharma[42] teacher-in-

---

[40] Ibid

[41] Sangha, which is one of the "Three Refuges", refers to a community of monks, nuns, novices and laity who practice the dharma together.

[42] "In Buddhism, dharma is the doctrine, the universal truth common to all individuals at all times, proclaimed by the Buddha," definition accessed at *Encyclopedia Britannica* at *Britannica.com*

training. He was also teaching large mindful yoga classes weekly in a church in Harvard Square and teaching yoga/stretching and meditation to athletes.[43]

This led to what he describes as a "strong impulse on my part . . . to bring my dharma practice together with my work life into one unified whole, as an expression of right livelihood and in the service of something useful that felt very much needed in the world."[44]

This strong impulse came to a head in 1979 when he had a powerful mystical experience on a two-week vipassana[45] retreat that instantly revealed how to go about this integration.

"[W]hile sitting in my room one afternoon about Day 10 of the retreat, I had a 'vision' that lasted maybe 10 seconds. . ... I saw in a flash not only a model that could be put in place, but also the long-term implications of what might happen if the basic idea was sound and could be implemented in one test environment — namely that it would spark new fields of scientific and clinical investigation, and would spread to hospitals and medical centers and clinics across the country and around the world and provide right livelihood for thousands of practitioners. Because it was so weird, I hardly ever mentioned this experience to others. But after that retreat, I did have a better sense of what my karmic assignment might be. It was so compelling that I decided to take it on wholeheartedly as best I could."[46]

---

[43]Kabat-Zinn, Jon, Ph.D., "Some Reflections on the Origins of MBSR," *Contemporary Buddhism, Vol. 12, No. 1,* May 2011, pg. 287
[44]Ibid, pg. 286
[45]According to the *Oxford English Dictionary*, vipassana is a style of meditation in the Theravada Buddhist tradition that involves concentration on the body or its sensations, or the insight this provides. Accessed at *oxforddictionaries.com*
[46]"Some Reflections on the Origins of MBSR," pg. 287

It occurred to him that he could share the essence of the meditation and yoga practices he had been learning with people who would never come to a place like the Zen Center by making meditation so commonsensical that anyone would be drawn to it.

"Why not develop an American[47] vocabulary that spoke to the heart of the matter, and didn't focus on the cultural aspects of the traditions out of which the dharma emerged . . . not because they weren't ultimately important, but because they would likely cause unnecessary impediments for people who were basically dealing with suffering and seeking some kind of release from it."[48]

Zinn believed the "naming" of something was very important in how it would be understood and decided to use an umbrella term for the program that was developing in his mind that would be palatable to the cultural climate of 1979 America. *Stress reduction* seemed to be an ideal choice because almost anyone can relate to it. And this name would remain true to its Buddhist roots in that some Buddhist scholars translate the term "dukkha," which means "suffering" or "sorrow" in Pali, as "stress."

In the spring of 1979, after experiencing the vision at the retreat, Zinn met with three physicians at the hospital who were directors of

---

[47]Zinn notes that at the time he used the word "American" but might now use the term "secular," except that it implies separating itself from the sacred. "I see the world of MBSR as sacred as well as secular, in the sense of both the Hippocratic Oath and the Bodhisattva Vow being sacred, and the doctor/patient relationship and the teacher/student relationship as well. . ... Each country and culture will have its own challenges in shaping the language to its own heart-essence without denaturing the wholeness of the dharma." "Some Reflections on the Origins of MBSR," Footnote #5 on page 301.
[48]Ibid

primary care, pain, and orthopedic clinics. He interviewed them to determine how they viewed their work and what was their success. When asked what percentage of patients they felt they were able to help, he was surprised that the typical response was just 10 to 20 percent. What happened to the rest? "I was told that they either got better on their own, or never got better."[49]

Zinn asked if they would be open to referring their patients to a program that would teach them how to take better care of themselves as a complement to whatever the healthcare system was doing. "It would be based on relatively intensive training in Buddhist meditation without the Buddhism (as I liked to put it), and yoga. Their response was very positive."[50]

MBSR officially came into being and word quickly spread through the hospital, then beyond into the larger medical community. Within a year, it became part of the Department of Medicine and thus entered the mainstream.

MBSR is now described as "a well-defined and systematic patient-centered educational approach which uses relatively intensive training in mindfulness meditation as the core of a program to teach people how to take better care of themselves and live healthier and more adaptive lives."[51]

The practice begins with a two-and-a-half-hour orientation session and personal interview followed by eight weekly classes of between two-

---

[49]"Some Reflections on the Origins of MBSR," pg. 293

[50]Ibid, pg. 294

[51]Kabat-Zinn, Jon Ph.D., Mindfulness Based Stress Reduction Standards of Practice, Center for Mindfulness in Medicine, Health Care & Society, Department of Medicine Division of Preventive and Behavioral Medicine, February 2014

and-a-half and three-and-a-half-hours' duration. Participants practice formal mindfulness meditation methods such as Body Scan Meditation. Gentle Hatha Yoga is practiced with "mindful awareness of the body." Sitting Meditation, which involves mindfulness of breath, body, feelings, thoughts, emotions, and "choiceless" awareness is also practiced along with walking meditation. Students are required to practice "informal" mindfulness meditation outside of the classroom, which entails mindfulness in everyday life. This involves awareness of pleasant and unpleasant events, awareness of breathing, deliberate awareness of routine activities and events such as: eating, weather, driving walking, and awareness of interpersonal communications. Daily home assignments include a minimum of forty-five minutes per day of formal mindfulness practice and five to fifteen minutes of informal practice, six days per week for the duration of the course. Another important component of MBSR is individual and group dialogue, which is oriented around weekly home assignments. In addition to the above requirements, an all-day (seven-and-a-half-hour) retreat during the sixth week of the program is required.[52]

It was nine years later that Kabat-Zinn's encounter with Thich Nhất Hanh would bring about a dramatic change in direction in his life. At the time, he was writing *Full Catastrophe Living: Using the Wisdom of Your Body and Mind to Face Stress, Pain and Illness* (*Delta*, 1991) and was struggling to capture the essence and spirit of the MBSR curriculum. The problem was how to articulate the dharma that underlies the curriculum without using the world "dharma" or invoking Buddhist thought or authority because this was not mentioned in typical MBSR

---

[52] Ibid

classes.

In the introduction to the book, he explicitly stated its Buddhist origins, but until then he had "bent over backward" to find ways to speak about it that avoided the risk of it being seen as Buddhist or "New Age", or defined as "Eastern Mysticism."

"To my mind, this was a constant and serious risk that would have undermined our attempts to present it as commonsensical, evidence-based, and ordinary, and ultimately a legitimate element of mainstream medical care. This was something of an ongoing challenge, given that the entire curriculum is based on relatively (for novices) intensive training and practice of meditation and yoga, and meditation and yoga pretty much defined one element of the 'New Age'."

Zinn was actively seeking colleagues that he respected who might want to endorse the book, and among those who were asked was Thich Nhất Hanh whom he had never met but whose writings he had long admired. Zinn wrote to him to explain the direction he was taking and to get Nhất Hanh's opinion of it. He was surprised to receive a response, which turned out to be a "gift" as it revealed just how much Nhất Hanh understood the essence of the book. It was so poignant that Zinn felt it would be disrespectful if he did not use it. But there was one big problem. Nhất Hanh did not share the same reservations as he did about using overt Buddhist terminology in describing MBSR.

"It precipitated something of a crisis in me for a time, because not only was Thich Nhất Hanh definitely a Buddhist authority, his brief endorsement used the very foreign word 'dharma' not once, but four times. . . I wondered: 'Is this the right time for this? Would it be skillful to stretch the envelope at this point? Or would it in the end cause more harm than good. In retrospect, these concerns now sound a bit silly to me. But at the time, they felt significant."[53]

Zinn eventually resolved his concerns by gambling on the fact that his original reservations had become a bit outdated. By 1990, there was no longer such a deep chasm between the New Age and mainstream America. Many counter-cultural trends were infiltrating the popular culture and even commonplace advertising was commercializing movements such as yoga and meditation, thereby breaking down many of the conventional stereotypes of previous years. He decided to take a chance and use Thich Nhất Hanh's words in the preface to the book.

His gamble paid off and MBSR entered the mainstream, spawning scientific investigations which accelerated the "confluence of dharma with mainstream medicine, healthcare, cognitive science, affective neuroscience, neuroeconomics, business, leadership, primary and secondary education, higher education, the law, indeed, in society as a whole, in this now very rapidly changing world."[54]

Kabat-Zinn is the author of numerous scientific papers on the clinical applications of mindfulness in medicine and health care as well as a number of books for the lay public:

- *Full Catastrophe Living: Using the Wisdom of Your Body and Mind to Face Stress, Pain and Illness* (Delta, 1991)
- *Wherever You Go, There You Are: Mindfulness Meditation in Everyday Life* (Hyperion, 1994)
- *Coming to Our Senses: Healing Ourselves and the World Through Mindfulness* (Hyperion, 2005)
- *Arriving at Your Own Door: 108 Lessons in Mindfulness*

---

[53] Ibid, pg. 283
[54] Ibid, pg. 284

(Hyperion, 2007)

- (With his wife Myla) *Everyday Blessings: The Inner Work of Mindful Parenting* (Hyperion, 1997) and

- (With Williams, Teasdale, and Segal) *The Mindful Way Through Depression: Freeing Yourself from Chronic Unhappiness* (Guilford, 2007).

Overall, his books have been translated into over thirty languages.[55]

Kabat-Zinn succeeded in bringing mindfulness into the American lexicon, a goal that he had in mind from the very beginning. He describes his primary motivation for bringing mindfulness into the mainstream of society as being a way to relieve suffering and "catalyze compassion and wisdom in our lives and culture."[56]

Secondary motivations include the potential for "elucidating and deepening our understanding of the mind/body connection via new dimensions of scientific investigation, and also the possibility of developing a form of right livelihood for myself at a particular juncture in my life, as well as . . . possibly large numbers of others . . ."[57]

And there was also the fact of "being in love with the beauty, simplicity, and universality of the dharma, and coming to see it as a worthy and meaningful pathway for a life well lived . . ."[58]

For Kabat-Zinn, the introduction of mindfulness into the American mind-set, as well as the program he developed, was always about much more than just the relief of suffering. Even his patients realized this and

---

[55] Faculty Profile, University of Massachusetts Medical School, Center for Mindfulness in Medicine, Healthcare and Society.
[56] "Some Reflections on the Origins of MBSR," pg. 285
[57] Ibid, pg. 286
[58] Ibid

would often explain, "This isn't stress reduction. This is my whole life."[59]

As for instructors of MBSR, Kabat-Zinn believed that it would be "hugely helpful" if they had a strong personal grounding in the Buddhadharma and its teachings. "In fact, it is virtually essential and indispensable for teachers of MBSR and other mindfulness-based interventions. Yet little or none of it can be brought into the classroom *except in essence.* And if the essence is absent, then whatever one is doing or thinks one is doing, it is certainly not mindfulness-based in the way we understand the term."

In other words, the Buddhist context was to remain, but was to be kept out of sight.

The approach Kabat-Zinn took to introduce mindfulness into the American mainstream is not at all out-of-sync with Buddhist methods of spreading the philosophy. In fact, it is in keeping with a long-standing Buddhist approach called *upaya*, which is usually translated as "expedient means" and derives from the Buddha's way of always addressing the person he is talking to in the language and frame of reference of that person.

"Buddhist teachers after the Buddha have continued that way so you see Chinese Buddhism explained in a very Chinese way and Tibetan Buddhism in a Tibetan style. This accounts for a proliferation of styles, texts and colors. Jon Kabat-Zinn has done nothing else but continue that tradition and restate the teaching in a way that makes it acceptable to the medical and the scientific world. . . All this is very traditionally Buddhist,

---

[59] Ibid, pg. 289

the product of upaya."[60]

As of this writing, a whole "family" of mindfulness-based interventions have sprung up, including Mindfulness-Based Cognitive Therapy (MBCT) which was developed by Dr. Zindel Segal, Distinguished Professor of Psychology in Mood Disorders at the University of Toronto, Dr. Mark Williams, Professor of Clinical Psychology at the University of Oxford, and research scientist Dr. John Teasdale. MBCT combines meditative practices and attitudes based on the cultivation of mindfulness for people who suffer repeat bouts of depression or chronic unhappiness.[61]

Mindfulness-Based Relapse Prevention (MBRP) was developed at the Addictive Behaviors Research Center at the University of Washington for people struggling to recover from addictive behaviors.[62]

Jean L. Kristeller, PhD, a clinical psychologist who earned her doctorate at Yale, began developing Mindfulness-Based Eating Awareness Training (MB-EAT) over fifteen years ago, and drew on her work with Kabat-Zinn's Mindfulness Based Stress Reduction program and on her research and clinical training in food intake regulation and eating disorders in designing the program.[63] As proponents of MB-EAT profess, "Mindfulness can help bring balance into every aspect of how we eat. It involves cultivating a combination of 'inner wisdom' (awareness of how our body and mind are responding), and 'outer

---

[60]Maex, Edele, "The Buddhist Roots of Mindfulness Training," Prifysgol Bangor University, Centre for Mindfulness Research and Practice, accessed at www.bangor.ac.uk.

[61]MBCT.com

[62]Mindfulrp.com

[63]The Center for Mindful Eating at thecenterformindfuleating.org

wisdom' (engaging nutrition information and recommendations to meet your own personal needs and preferences)."[64]

How effective are these programs? Are they safe? Have they been scientifically tested? The following chapter will attempt to answer these questions.

---

[64] Mindful Eating website at mb-eat.com

Chapter Three

The Science of Mindfulness

When it comes to the scientific study of mindfulness, researchers warn that there are many caveats to take into consideration before adopting the prevailing view that mindfulness is the next best thing to a cure for cancer.

Catherine Wikholm, a researcher in clinical psychology at the University of Surrey who participated in a 2015 study of mindfulness and meditation, summed up these precautions very succinctly: "It is hard to have a balanced view when the media is full of articles attesting to the benefits of meditation and mindfulness. We need to be aware that reports of benefits are often inflated ... whereas studies that do not discover significant benefits rarely pick up media interest, and negative effects are seldom talked about."[65]

Wilkholm and fellow psychologist Miguel Farias authored a book on the subject, entitled *The Buddha Pill: Can Meditation Change You?*

---

[65] Wikholm, Catherine, "The Dark Side of Meditation and Mindfulness: Treatment can trigger mania, depression and psychosis, new book claims," *Daily Mail*, May 22, 2015

which puts the subject of mindfulness and meditation under a microscope. It presents ground-breaking studies on the impact of these and other eastern techniques, including the unexpected consequences of the pursuit of personal change.

The book is indeed timely. There is an ever-burgeoning collection of research — almost all of it positive — that alleges dozens of physical health benefits of mindfulness, such as improving brain and immune system function, lowering blood pressure, improving sleep, treating binge eating and even reducing the pace of cellular aging. Mental health benefits are even more impressive with research suggesting the practice of mindfulness can reduce stress and anxiety, improve concentration and focus, treat depression and various personality and bi-polar disorders.

Let's take a look at some of the most publicized areas of research.

Stress and Anxiety

By far, the most prolific area of study is in the treatment of stress and anxiety. In a 2010 meta-analysis of thirty-nine studies that explored the use of mindfulness-based stress reduction (MBSR) and mindfulness-based cognitive therapy (MBCT) on stress-related conditions, "researchers concluded that mindfulness-based therapy may be useful in altering affective and cognitive processes that underlie multiple clinical issues."[66]

In one of the studies included in the analysis, participant responses

---

[66] Davis, Daphne M. PhD, and Hayes, Jeffrey A. PhD, "What are the Benefits of Mindfulness?" American Psychological Association, July/August 2012, Vol. 43, No. 7

were measured on levels of depression, anxiety and psychopathology, and neural reactivity as measured by fMRI after participants watched sad movies. One group was randomly assigned to an eight-week mindfulness-based stress reduction group and the other was not.

"The researchers found that the participants who experienced mindfulness-based stress reduction had significantly less anxiety, depression and somatic distress compared with the control group. In addition, the fMRI data indicated that the mindfulness group had less neural reactivity when they were exposed to the films than the control group, and they displayed distinctly different neural responses while watching the films than they did before their mindfulness training."[67]

These findings suggest that mindfulness meditation enables people to better regulate and experience emotions, and to do so in a way that may be processed differently in the brain than those not engaged in the practice.

MBSR has also been used to treat Generalized Anxiety Disorder (GAD), a condition where people worry excessively over everyday activities, in some cases to the point of experiencing panic attacks, even when there is no cause for concern, which gives them a poor quality of life.

Researchers found that through the practice of mindfulness, the constant awareness of the present moment interrupts the thoughts that would otherwise elicit feelings of fear that precipitate panic attacks.

"Thus mindfulness refocuses thoughts and helps anxious individuals focus on the present moment instead of their feelings of worry. . .. This suggests that the mindfulness component of MBSR would help anxious

---

[67] Ibid

individuals be aware of their present thoughts, thus preventing panic attacks and making it easier for them to live their day to day lives . . ."[68]

According to Dr. Elizabeth Hoge, a psychiatrist at the Center for Anxiety and Traumatic Stress Disorders at Massachusetts General Hospital and an assistant professor of psychiatry at Harvard Medical School, mindfulness meditation makes perfect sense for treating anxiety.[69]

"People with anxiety have a problem dealing with distracting thoughts that have too much power. They can't distinguish between a problem-solving thought and a nagging worry that has no benefit," Dr. Hoge explained.

For example, if a person has an unproductive worry, mindfulness teaches them to train themselves to experience the thoughts that precipitated the worry in a different way.

"You might think 'I'm late, I might lose my job if I don't get there on time, and it will be a disaster!' Mindfulness teaches you to recognize, 'Oh, there's that thought again. I've been here before. But it's just that — a thought, and not a part of my core self,'" she continues.

Dr. Hoge conducted a high-quality study which found that a mindfulness-based stress reduction program helped quell anxiety symptoms in people with GAD.

Even though researchers have not yet studied the effects of mindfulness practice on people suffering from post-traumatic stress disorder (PTSD), meditation programs are being used to help reduce the

---

[68] Sethi, Prairna, "The Effects of Mindfulness on Anxiety and Aggression," *OPUS*, Department of Applied Psychology, New York University/Steinhardt
[69] Corliss, Julie, "Mindfulness Meditation May Ease Anxiety, Mental Stress," *Harvard Health Publications*, Harvard Medical School, December 14, 2016

severity of the condition in veterans.

"Mindfulness practices may be of benefit to trauma survivors. Research findings show that mindfulness can help with problems and symptoms often experienced by survivors. Mindfulness could be used by itself or together with standard treatments proven effective for PTSD."[70]

Mental Health Conditions & Depression

Research has found that mindfulness and acceptance-based interventions can be useful additions to other treatments for improving symptoms as well as reducing hospitalization among people with psychosis.

Mindfulness-based programs for the treatment of depression have also received much attention from the scientific community. In one study, published in the *Journal of the American Medical Association* in 2010, MBCT prevented recurring depression episodes in eighty-four people in remission just as well as medication and better than a placebo.

There is also evidence that MBCT is more helpful to patients who are more vulnerable to relapse into depression, such as those who suffered a greater number of prior episodes. MBCT was found to be more effective in preventing relapse among people with three or more episodes, reducing risk by forty-three percent versus thirty-four percent for participants overall.

Another group that was found to be more likely to benefit from MBCT were those who suffered depression at an earlier age, or who

---

[70]"Mindfulness Practice in the Treatment of Traumatic Stress," National Center for PTSD

were subjected to abuse or other adversity in their childhoods.

In another study, participants who had depression at earlier ages, or who had more adversity or abuse in childhood, were found to be more likely to benefit from MBCT, perhaps because the patients were more motivated and invested in the treatment.

"They've been depressed more, they've had all these unpleasant things happening to them and they've often tried antidepressants and other kinds of therapy, so they're willing to meditate forty minutes a day and to do something quite different in terms of mindfulness practices like mindful movement," said Willem Kuyken, PhD, a professor at the University of Oxford in the United Kingdom. "Those who do best are those ready to engage fully."[71]

Even though the evidence suggests mindfulness works to help prevent depression relapse, researchers don't yet know how.

"It may be that mindfulness leads to an increase in self-compassion and a decrease in experiential avoidance," says Stuart Eisendrath, MD, professor and head of the Depression Center at the University of California, San Francisco. "It may be selective attention — if you focus on your breath, you have less bandwidth to ruminate. There are a lot of factors that are operative and we're just beginning to tease out and deconstruct them. It's like tasting a soup with 10 spices. Is there one main ingredient or is the flavor a combination of things?"[72]

One characteristic of depression is a habit of thinking negatively about oneself, an experience, or the future. "Mindfulness trains people

---

[71] Lu, Stacy, "Mindfulness Holds Promise for Treating Depression," American Psychological Association, 2015, *Vol. 46, No. 3*, page 50
[72] Ibid

to be more aware of these thoughts and to stand back and simply observe their thoughts passing through their minds — 'Oh, there I go again, calling myself an idiot' — instead of trying to control their emotions. Or, in the case of people who have recovered from depression, blaming themselves for feeling down again or worrying about a relapse."[73]

MBCT's emphasis on cultivating awareness and acceptance of the present moment also serves to harness ruminating or wandering thoughts, both of which are implicated in depression.

Other research has found that mindfulness-based treatment is effective in preventing relapses into depression for those in remission. In one study, researchers found that 37 percent of those that went through an eight-week MBCT program experienced a relapse compared to 66 percent of those not in the program.[74]

Some of these good results could be due to the fact that mindfulness meditation has been shown to affect how the brain works. "People undertaking mindfulness training have shown increased activity in the area of the brain associated with positive emotion — the pre-frontal cortex — which is generally less active in people who are depressed."[75]

Another program, mindfulness-based relapse prevention (MBRP) which was designed to treat substance use disorder, integrates

---

[73] Ibid

[74] Flaxman, Greg and Flook, Lisa PhD, "Brief Summary of Mindfulness Research," UCLA Mindful Awareness Research Center

[75] "Mindfulness," Mental Health Foundation, citing Kerr, C. et al. (2013), "Mindfulness starts with the body: somatosensory attention and top-down modulation of cortical alpha rhythms in mindfulness meditation." *Frontiers in Human Neuroscience, 7.*

mindfulness meditation and cognitive-behavior skills to help patients learn how to choose a reaction instead of turning to an addictive substance.

"Research comparing mindfulness-based relapse prevention with other treatment for aftercare found it to be effective and particularly useful in supporting longer-term benefits of treatment. In the study patients with mindfulness-based relapse prevention treatment had significantly less drug use and a lower probability of any heavy drinking at a 12-month follow-up than those undergoing other treatments."[76]

Relationships

Aside from possible mental and physical benefits of mindfulness training, research has also focused on examining how this practice may benefit social and familial relationships.

In one study, conducted at the University of North Carolina at Chapel Hill, researchers found a correlation between mindfulness practice in couples to improved closeness, acceptance of one another, autonomy, and general relationship satisfaction. This research was later replicated in another study, which found a correlation between mindfulness and the quality of communication between romantic partners.[77]

Research has also found that mindfulness practice can benefit familial relationships. For instance, two studies found that parents of children with developmental disabilities felt increased satisfaction with

---

[76] APA Staff, "Mindfulness Practices May Help Treat Many Mental Disorders," American Psychiatric Association, *APA Blog*, June 1, 2016,
[77] "Brief Summary of Mindfulness Research," pg. 2

their parenting, and had more social interactions with their children and less parenting stress.

"In both studies, the children of these parents benefited from the mindful parenting practice, showing decreases in aggressive and non-compliant behavior. In addition, a mindfulness intervention for adolescents with externalizing disorders that involved their parents in the treatment showed improvement in the happiness of the children, as well as the parents' perception of their child's self-control."[78]

Education

Researchers are also studying the impact of mindfulness programs on students.

"Two pilot studies conducted through UCLA's Mindful Awareness Research Center indicate improvements in self-regulatory abilities among preschool and elementary school students who participated in an eight-week mindful awareness practices training program (developed and taught by InnerKids in two 30-minute sessions per week). Specifically, children who were initially less well-regulated showed the strongest improvements subsequent to training, as compared to children in the control group who did not receive the training."[79]

While the above exposé of some of the major research done to date on the impact of mindfulness on the mental and physical health of participants might sound impressive, only a small percentage of this research is considered to be of acceptable quality.

---

[78] Ibid, pg. 3
[79] Ibid, pg. 5

Studies Called into Question

In 2014, researchers at Johns Hopkins University in Baltimore, Maryland reviewed nearly 19,000 meditation studies and came up with only forty-seven that met their criteria for a well-designed study.

As the researchers explain: "These reviews have largely included uncontrolled and controlled studies, and many of the controlled studies did not adequately control for placebo effects (e.g., waiting list — or usual care — controlled studies). Observational studies have a high risk of bias owing to problems such as self-selection of interventions (people who believe in the benefits of meditation or who have prior experience with meditation are more likely to enroll in a meditation program and report that they benefited from one) and use of outcome measures that can be easily biased by participants' beliefs in the benefits of meditation. Clinicians need to know whether meditation training has beneficial effects beyond self-selection biases and the nonspecific effects of time, attention, and expectations for improvement."[80]

Of the forty-seven studies that made the cut, "Reviews to date report a small to moderate effect of mindfulness and mantra meditation techniques [i.e. transcendental meditation] in reducing emotional symptoms (e.g., anxiety, depression, and stress) and improving physical symptoms (e.g., pain) . . . We found no evidence that meditation programs were better than any active treatment (i.e., drugs, exercise, and

---

[80] Goyal, Madav, MD, MPH; Singh, Sonal MD, MPH; Sibinga, Erica M.S., MD, MPH, "Meditation Programs for Psychological Stress and Well-Being: A Systematic Review and Meta-Analysis, *JAMA Internal Medicine*, 2014; 174(3): 357-368

other behavioral therapies)."[81]

Specifically, the research found only "moderate evidence" of improved anxiety, depression and pain as a result of mindfulness based programs and "low evidence" of improved stress/distress and mental health-related quality of life. However, they found enough evidence to warrant more study.

In other words, the effect of mindfulness-based interventions is not nearly as spectacular as the mainstream media tends to report it.

And as the same paper goes on to warn, even though they found no evidence of any harms of meditation programs, this wasn't due to the fact that there aren't any — only that there were too few trials that reported on these harms.

This criticism has been echoed by other serious researchers, such as Utpal Dholakia, Ph.D., who questions why the so-called rapid success of mindfulness meditation into the mainstream has done so little to affect the prevailing mindlessness of society.

"Virtually every major Silicon Valley firm — whether it is Google, Twitter, Facebook, or LinkedIn — now offers mindfulness training as a perk for its employees. Even hard-nosed financial institutions like Goldman Sachs have climbed on board the mindfulness bandwagon. What is more, mindfulness programs have percolated into American prisons, the military, and are part of curricula in numerous schools and universities throughout the country," he writes.[82]

So why isn't it working? He cites the recent increases in fatalities and

---

[81] Ibid

[82] Dholakia, Utpal, PhD, "If Mindfulness is so Popular, Why is Everyone so Mindless?" *Psychology Today*, April 4, 2016

accidents due to distracted driving, the compulsion to constantly check smartphones, the mindless eating, and even the crisis of opioid drug addiction — all of which has reduced the attention span of the average American from twelve seconds in 2000 to eight seconds in 2015.[83]

With all the hype about mindfulness, it obviously isn't translating into a more mindful society.

Even though Dholakia occasionally practices mindfulness himself, he feels compelled to draw attention to the emerging research that points to potentially negative consequences of the practice, evidence that is too often swept under the rug in what has been to date a very unbalanced portrayal of mindfulness.

One of the most astonishing examples he cites is a paper published in 2009 in *Advances in Mind-Body Medicine* in which a team of researchers led by psychologist Kathleen Lustyk found a long list of psychological and physical side effects of mindfulness meditation. These include depersonalization, which is the feeling of being detached from one's mental processes or body, and psychosis, which is the loss of contact with reality accompanied by delusions. Additional negative effects include hallucinations, disorganized speech, feelings of anxiety, an increased risk of seizures, loss of appetite and insomnia.[84]

"Their main point was that participants should be screened carefully for their suitability before undertaking this practice, and its teachers should be properly trained and supervised," Dholakia reports.

---

[83] Ibid

[84] Lustyk, M. Kathleen B.; Chawla, Neharika, MS; Nolan, Roger S., MA; Marlatt, G. Alan, PhD, "Mindfulness Meditation Research: Issues of Participant Screening, Safety Procedures and Researcher Training," *Advances in Mind-Body Medicine*, Spring 2009, Vol. 24, No. 1

As shocking as this research may sound, it's not new. A 1992 study by David Shapiro, a professor at the University of California, Irvine, found that 63 percent of the group he studied, who had varying degrees of experience in meditation and had each tried mindfulness, had suffered at least one negative effect from meditation retreats. Seven percent reported profoundly adverse effects including panic, depression, pain, and anxiety. Even though Shapiro's study was considered to be small-scale, researchers are continuing to raise the alarm about the lack of high-quality research on the negative impact of mindfulness.[85]

This was certainly the case with Wikholm, who provides plenty of evidence of negative effects in *The Buddha Pill,* such as the research conducted on inmates at seven prisons in the British Midlands. In this study, participants attended ninety-minute classes once a week and completed tests to measure their higher cognitive functions in a ten-week randomized control trial.

"The prisoners' moods improved, and their stress and psychological distress reduced — but they were found to be just as aggressive before the mindfulness techniques."[86]

Some of these adverse effects could be due to the fact that mindfulness meditation can induce an altered state of consciousness, which occurs when there is a temporary change in one's normal mental state. This can happen as a result of high fevers, drugs, coma, sleep or oxygen deprivation, or eastern meditation practices that call for the deliberate blanking of the mind through some kind of concentration

---

[85] Foster, Dawn, "Is Mindfulness Making Us Ill?" *The Guardian,* January 23, 2016
[86] Crawford, Harriet, "The Dark Side of Meditation and Mindfulness: Treatment can Trigger Mania, Depression and Psychosis, New Book Claims," *The Daily Mail,* May 22, 2015

exercise either by focusing on a mantra or breathing. These practices include transcendental meditation, yoga, mindfulness meditation, centering prayer, hypnosis, and other similar techniques. Typical side effects range from psychotic-like delusional thinking and panic attacks to insomnia and outright personality changes. Antisocial acting out, loss of concentration, confusion, impaired coping skills, and depression can all occur in the wake of an induced altered state.

For example, the authors found that one in fourteen people who practiced these meditation methods suffered "profoundly adverse effects" that include mania, hallucinations and psychosis — all of which are known side effects of deliberately-altered mental states.

"The assumption of the majority of both TM [transcendental meditation] and mindfulness researchers is that meditation can only do one good," said Dr. Miquel Farias, co-author of *The Buddha Pill,* who serves as head of the brain, belief, and behavior research group at the UK's Coventry University.

"This shows a rather narrow-minded view. How can a technique that allows you to look within and change your perception or reality of yourself be without potential adverse effects? The answer is that it can't, and all meditation studies should assess not only positive but negative effects."

Perhaps this is why the use of mindfulness, which is a practice aimed at restraining the senses by remaining focused on a nonjudgmental awareness of the present moment, has been found to actually reduce empathy in some populations.

"While there was no overall effect on empathy in the mindfulness group, further analysis revealed that, compared with the control and relaxation groups combined, non-narcissists who completed the mindfulness exercise did show a slight improvement specifically in cognitive empathy, but for narcissistic people, their cognitive empathy was actually reduced."[87]

The list of adverse effects continues. Dohlakia reports on another problem associated with the practice of mindfulness such as the one outlined in a study published in *Psychological Science*.[88] Researchers found that after a single fifteen-minute mindfulness exercise involving guided breathing, participants were more likely to form false memories compared to a control group who engaged in mind-wandering. Researchers called the formation of fake memories "a potential unintended consequence of mindfulness meditation in which memories become less reliable."[89]

Another possible unintended consequence of mindfulness meditation has to do with the discarding of positive thoughts along with the negative. This comes about due to the practice of learning how to separate from one's thoughts, then discarding all thoughts seen as negative or harmful. In a paper published by psychologist Pablo Brinol, it was found that when participants engaged in a ritual of discarding of thoughts such as by writing them down and then throwing them away, participants were also throwing away positive thoughts. The authors caution: "This finding suggests that techniques involved in some

---

[87] Young, Emma, "Brief Mindfulness practice does not foster empathy, and can even make narcissists worse," *Research Digest*, The British Psychological Society, May 17, 2017

[88] Wilson, Brent M.; Mickes, Laura; Stolarz-Fantino, Stephanie; Evrard, Matthew; Fantino, Edmund, "False Memory Susceptibility After Mindfulness Meditation," *Psychological Science*, September 4, 2015.

[89] Dholkia, Utpal, PhD, "The Little-Known Downsides of Mindfulness Practice," *Psychology Today*, April 26, 2016

mindfulness treatments can backfire — at least for some people and for some situations, particularly those in which positive thoughts are present."[90]

As Dohlakia points out, when we try to cull our negative baggage with mindfulness practice, "we may find we have left behind some precious and strengthening baggage with it."[91]

Another issue concerns those who use the practice of mindfulness to escape from the challenges of life. Psychiatrist David Brendel explains how his enthusiasm for mindfulness has been tempered by his increasing knowledge of, and experience with, its potential excesses.

"Some people use mindfulness strategies to avoid critical thinking tasks. I've worked with clients who, instead of rationally thinking through a career challenge or ethical dilemma, prefer to disconnect from their challenges and retreat into a meditative mindset. The issue here is that some problems require more thinking, not less."[92]

He tries to tell his patients that sometimes stress is a signal that they need to devote more thought to a situation rather than retreat into focused breathing. "Mindfulness strategies can prime the mind for sounder rational thinking — but the former clearly should not displace the latter."

Dr. Brendel refers to one client who spent so much time meditating and "mindfully" accepting her life "on its own terms" that she failed to

---

[90] Brinol, Pablo; Gasco, Margarita; Petty, Richard E.; Horcajo, Javier, "Treating Thoughts as Material Objects Can Increase or Decrease Their Impact on Evaluation," *Psychological Science*, November 26, 2012

[91] "The Little-Known Downsides of Mindfulness Practice"

[92] Brendel, David, MD, PhD, "There Are Risks to Mindfulness at Work," *Harvard Business Review*, February 11, 2015

confront underperforming workers in her company.

"After periods of meditating, she struggled to return to focused, task-oriented thinking. She required significant reminders and reassurance from me that embracing Buddhist meditation does not entail tolerating substandard performance from her employees. Mindful meditation should always be used in the service of enhancing, not displacing, people's rational and analytical thought processes about their careers and personal lives."

Even more concerning are other effects of mindfulness that are not being addressed such as what seems to be the development of clairaudience, psychokinesis, telepathic knowledge and clairvoyance in practitioners.

Dr. Kim Penberthy, Chester F. Carlson Professor of Psychiatry and Neurobehavioral Sciences at the University of Virginia Division of Perceptual Studies, presented these little-known effects of mindfulness practice at a public lecture which took place at the Boston Museum of Science on September 17, 2016. It was part of a special one-day event entitled, "Do We Survive Death? A Look at the Evidence."

In her presentation, she cited research[93] into increased psi [psychic] activity in meditators ranging from clairvoyance and telepathy to clairaudience and psychokinesis, which she described as one of the most exciting parts of her presentation.

"There are a few of us who are beginning to wake up to this. We need to collect this information. If you go back to some of their original literature grounded in spiritual context in which it started, these are to

---

[93] Roney-Dougal, Serena; Ryan, Adrian; Luke, David, "The Relationship Between Local Geomagnetic Activity, Meditation and Psi. Part I: Literature Review and Theoretical Model 1,

be expected and in some cases this would be the whole point of your mindfulness meditation so why are we ignoring it?"

She went on to cite one study of 1,120 meditators which found 50 percent of participants self-reporting that they almost always, or many times, had extraordinary experiences while meditating. Another 50 percent endorsed clairvoyance and telepathy.

"These are huge numbers! To outside scientists, these are mind-boggling," she said.

"What we're doing is trying to move forward to the next step to look at these practices and use them . . . intentionally to see if we can generate these qualities. We're looking at psi abilities in very scientific ways to see if we can create this and expand the method of achievement of the mindfulness state, and then accessing these abilities and exploring the impact of that. If we can increase that in a group of people what does that do to the community? What does that do to the individual? Can we take this to another level? . . . It's impressive to think about what we could do with these kinds of abilities if we put our mind to it and do it intentionally."

Before jumping on the mindfulness bandwagon, it would be wise to remember one important point about Buddhist meditation. It was not designed to make us happier, "but to radically change our sense of self and perception of the world."[94]

Which leads us to the most important question of all — should Catholics practice mindfulness?

---

[94]"Brief Summary of Mindfulness Research"

Chapter Four

Do Buddhism and Catholicism Mix?

Although some may argue that mindfulness, as it is practiced in the West, is not Buddhist, the preceding chapters should have sufficiently put that assertion to rest. The practice of mindfulness is so inextricably rooted in Buddhism, in fact, that one of the most prominent pioneers in the introduction of the practice to the West, Jon Kabat-Zinn, openly admits that he "bent over backward" to keep this truth hidden for fear of alienating the culturally Christian audience in the West.

Like many other cognitive-behavioral therapists, Kabat-Zinn insists that mindfulness is universal because it is nothing more than a particular method of paying attention; however, they can't escape the fact that their preferred method does indeed originate in the world's fourth-largest religion.

In fact, as we read in a previous chapter, the idea for the construction of what became the West's blueprint for mindfulness-based therapies was received by Kabat-Zinn during a religious experience at a Buddhist retreat.

This could explain why he was so conflicted about the Buddhist roots of his programs, conflicts which are evidenced by the instructions he gives to those who will teach MBSR. While insisting that it would be "hugely helpful" if MBSR instructors have a strong personal grounding in the Buddhadharma and its teachings, at the same time he insists that they be careful to bring only the essence of these Buddhist roots into the classroom.

Regardless of his personal conflict, Kabat-Zinn's approach raises ethical questions due to his insistence that both instructor and patient utilize a Buddhist practice while attempting to hide the spiritual roots of that practice. Even though exceptions are made at Kabat-Zinn's Center for Mindfulness for those who wish to engage in other forms of contemplation, his FAQ[95] sheet states that engaging in the prescribed mindfulness practices is "perhaps the most important component of the course." In other words, both patient and instructor are expected to embrace — or at least employ — Buddhist and other non-Christian eastern practices regardless of their own beliefs.

This won't be the first time that imposing religion on persons, particularly patients, under the guise of a therapy program, has garnered criticism from mental health experts.

"[C]lients are led to adopt religious or spiritual concepts in which they previously had no interest and which may run counter to their personal belief system. Although the clients thought they were seeking psychotherapy, they were in effect put through a religious

---

[95] University of Massachusetts Medical School, Center for Mindfulness in Medicine, Healthcare and Society, FAQs, accessed at http://www.umassmed.edu/cfm/mindfulness-based-programs/faqs-mbsr-mbct/

conversion. . ... Unexpectedly taking on this belief during the course of therapy can cause certain clients to experience upsetting internal conflict, and they may not recognize the source of their difficulty."[96]

This is important to note because regardless of whether or not the Buddhist roots are promoted, mindfulness as therapy overlaps with mindfulness as spirituality.

"Though mindfulness is often learned or practiced in a secular manner, individuals often report spiritual benefits from their practice. On the whole, research suggests that mindfulness and spirituality are overlapping but distinct constructs, that they likely interact and contribute to one another's development, and that both are important mechanisms through which MBIs [mindfulness-based interventions] exert benefits."[97]

This is especially true because mindfulness meditation is known to induce an altered state of consciousness.

For all of the above reasons, before we can consider whether or not the practice of mindfulness — either as therapy or meditation — is suitable for Catholics, we must first look at the religion in which it originates and confront a question that has caused controversy for decades — are Buddhism and Catholicism compatible?

---

[96] Singer, Margaret Thaler and Lalich Janja, *Crazy Therapies: What Are They? Do They Work?* (San Francisco, CA: Jossy-Bass Publishers, 1996) pg.19

[97] Kim-Preito, Chu, *Religion and Spirituality Across Cultures,* (New York, NY: Springer, 2014) quoting Chapter 11, "Mindfulness, Consciousness, Spirituality, and Well-Being" by Emily L. B. Lykons, pg. 203

Dialogue versus Syncretism

This question first arose in some Catholic circles during the 1960's in the wake of the Second Vatican Council's call for respectful dialogue with other religions. Although not encouraged by the Council, many Catholics began to look to the east for new forms of "prayer" and ethical codes, with Buddhism becoming a particularly popular choice.

"Much was made (and still is) of the many 'common characteristics' of Catholicism and Buddhism, especially in the realm of ethics," write Anthony E. Clark and Carl E. Olson. "External similarities, including monks, meditation, and prayer beads, seemed to indicate a newly discovered closeness between the followers of Christ and Buddha. While some helpful interreligious dialogue and study was accomplished, some Catholics mistakenly concluded that Buddhism was just as 'true' as Christianity, and that any criticism of Buddhism was 'arrogant' and 'triumphalistic'."[98]

This attitude has prevailed to the current day, which explains why so many Catholic retreat centers offer classes in eastern religious practices such as yoga, tai chi, Zen, et cetera.

Perhaps one of the most prevalent arguments in favor of the blending of Buddhism with Catholicism is the belief that Buddhism is not really a religion because it does not involve the worship of a god. Many believe it to be more of a philosophy or system of ethics similar to Confucianism. This dispute can even be found among the most devout

---

[98] Clark, Anthony E. and Olson, Carl E., "Catholicism and Buddhism," *Ignatius Insight*, February 5, 2005.

followers of Buddha.[99]

As Peter Kreeft, PhD, professor of philosophy at Boston College and The King's College notes, "Buddhism does not deny God. It is silent about God."[100]

However, it is also true that some Buddhists, such as the Pure Land sect, divinized Buddha.[101] Others believe he was the "teacher of gods and men." Some Buddhists believe in multiple deities that look after the affairs of men and nature. Still others point out that certain teachings of Buddha specifically point to an uncreated being without which nothing would be in existence.[102]

But for the most part, at least on the surface, Buddhism appears to be a simple "god-free" code of ethics that anyone can live by, whether they believe in a god or not.

"Because it is peaceful, non-judgmental, and inclusive, its appeal will undoubtedly continue to grow," warn Clark and Olson. "Because it offers a spirituality that is supposedly free of doctrine and authority, it will attract hungry souls looking for fulfillment and meaning."[103]

But for the Christian, its seemingly harmless façade wears away quickly upon closer inspection.

For example, the Buddhist might allow a person to believe in God or an afterlife, but this allowance is only a means to an end — what we

---

[99]Mirus, Peter, "Catholicism and Buddhism: Compatible Beliefs?", Catholicculture.org, August 29, 2006.

[100] Kreeft, Peter PhD, "Comparing Christianity & Buddhism," accessed at peterkreeft.com

[101] Ibid

[102] "Catholicism and Buddhism: Compatible Beliefs?"

[103] "Catholicism and Buddhism"

learned earlier is referred to in Buddhism as upaya. This is because, to a Buddhist, all religious belief is nothing more than a theory.

"According to Buddhist upaya, Christianity is allowable as long as it is viewed as a stage of spiritual progression, leading eventually to the extinction of self — nirvana."[104]

In other words, belief in the redemption of mankind in Jesus Christ is a mere human construct, not an eternal Truth.

No Soul, No Self

Buddhists do not believe in the existence of the soul in the same way Christians do, which is a major stumbling block for the Christian. Buddhists believe that people who think they have a permanent or eternal soul are rooted in ignorance and in a desire to please one's "self," and that we become truly enlightened only after we come to the realization that there is no such thing as an enduring soul.

Instead, Buddhism teaches the doctrine of the an-atta, or "no self", which is the belief that we are made of strands (*skandhas*) of interpersonal consciousness that are woven together by necessity without any underlying substance, self, or soul.[105]

"It's denial of soul has practical import: It teaches us not to be 'attached,' not to send our soul out in desire, not to love. Instead of personal, individual, free-willed agape (active love), Buddhism teaches an impersonal, universal feeling of compassion (*karuna*). . .. Karuna and agape lead the disciple to do similar, strikingly selfless deeds — but in

---

[104] Ibid

[105] "Comparing Christianity and Buddhism"

strikingly different spirits."[106]

Dr. Kreeft uses as an example a Buddhist story about a saint who gave his cloak to a beggar. The Buddhist's explanation was not because he loved the beggar or because Christ loves the beggar, but because "this is the enlightened thing to do. For if you were freezing and had two gloves on one hand and none on the other hand, would it not be the enlightened thing to do to give one of the gloves to the bare hand?"[107]

In other words, the Buddhist's concern is not for the welfare of the recipient, but for the liberation of the giver from the burden of self.

For that matter, not even the Buddhist notion of self is compatible with Christian belief. Just as there is no permanent soul, there is also no "self" because it's very existence is denied.

In Buddhist teaching, the individual man is made up of five *Skandhas* or "heaps": the Body, the Feelings, the Perceptions, the Impulses and Emotions, and the Acts of Consciousness.

"Each person is not someone endowed with these five "heaps"; he is these 'heaps,' the bundle of these Skandhas but without any permanent substratum or soul. In fact, there is no individuality at all. Individuality is only an invented belief, a product of gratuitous imagination, a grand delusion. The aim of the Dharma and the goal of the Middle Way is the extinguishing of belief in an individuality. When the individual ceases to exist, the result is 'extinction', Nirvana."[108]

Nirvana, then, is actually a negative concept because it means the extinction of the self, the end of the processes of karma and rebirth.

---

[106] Ibid

[107] Ibid

[108] Wilkinson, Rev. Peter J., "Buddhism: A Catholic Perspective," A.C.T.S. No. 1537 (1968)

The belief that individuality is an invented concept is radically dissimilar to Christian belief in the innate dignity of the human person.

As Pope St. John Paul II writes, "Human persons are willed by God; they are imprinted with God's image. Their dignity does not come from the work they do, but from the persons they are."[109]

The dramatic differences between the Buddhist and Christian concept of soul and self is perhaps most obvious when we consider the eastern belief in reincarnation, a process by which a person continually dies and is reborn until reaching a state of nirvana or the extinction of the self.

Even though its followers embrace this concept, this total annihilation of self is not the most palatable teaching to some Buddhists.

For example, Paul Williams, professor of Indian and Tibetan Philosophy at the University of Bristol in the UK who converted to Catholicism from Buddhism, says he was always unsettled by this teaching and the many facets of reincarnation that just didn't add up in his mind.

"[B]uddhists claim, there is no chronological first beginning to the series of past lives. We have all of us been reborn an infinite number of times. No God is needed to start the series off — for there simply was no first beginning. Things have been around (somewhere) for all eternity," Williams writes. He uses a hypothetical situation of a man being told that he will be executed in the morning; however, the man should not be terrified because he is going to come back as a cockroach in South America.

"My point is this: What is so terrifying about my being executed at

---

109 Pope St. John Paul II, *Centesimus Annus*, No. 11

dawn and reborn as a cockroach is that it is simply, quite straightforwardly, the end of me. I cannot imagine being reborn as a cockroach because there is nothing to imagine. I quite simply would not be there at all. If rebirth is true, neither I nor any of my loved ones survive death. With rebirth, for me — the actual person I am — the story really is over."[110]

Some Buddhists argue against this conclusion, claiming that the person is made up of thoughts, feelings and perceptions, all of which interact with the body in constantly changing ways. At death this stream of mental energy simply re-establishes itself in a new body.[111]

This does little to relieve Williams' discomfort. "There may be another being living its life in some sort of causal connection with the life that was me (influenced by my karma), but for me there is no more. That is it — the end of it. There is no more to be said about me."

Even though he does not believe this means the Buddhist position is wrong, it simply means that if it's correct then death is the end, a conclusion he finds to be utterly hopeless.

Reincarnation versus Resurrection

Regardless of this inherently hopeless teaching, recent studies have found a quarter of Americans believe in reincarnation, a number that

---

[110] Williams, Paul, "On Converting from Buddhism to Catholicism: One Convert's Story," accessed at whyimcatholic.com

[111] "Dharma Data: Rebirth," accessed at Buddhist Studies: Buddha Dharma Education Association at Buddhanet

certainly includes many Christians.[112]

One reason given by some Catholic believers in rebirth is that the Church has never officially condemned reincarnation. They believe this means reincarnation may one day be reconciled to the Christian concept of death and the afterlife.

However, as Cardinal Christoph Schonborn explains, the reason why the Church never condemned reincarnation is not because she may one day accept it as doctrine but "because reincarnation so obviously contradicts the very principles of this faith that a condemnation has never seemed necessary."[113]

Church teaching on this subject is quite clear. "Death is the end of man's earthly pilgrimage, of the time of grace and mercy which God offers him so as to work out his earthly life in keeping with the divine plan, and to decide his ultimate destiny. When 'the single course of our earthly life' is completed, we shall not return to other earthly lives: 'It is appointed for men to die once.' There is no 'reincarnation' after death."[114]

This teaching comes straight from Scripture in the Letter to the Hebrews, which responds to the question of whether or not there is more than one lifetime. It clearly states that it is "appointed for mortals to die once, and after that the judgment."[115]

---

[112] "Many Americans Mix Multiple Faiths," Pew Research Center, Religion and Public Life, December, 2009

[113] Schonborn, Cardinal Christoph, excerpt from *From Death to Life: A Christian Journey*, appearing on Ignatius Insight.com

[114] *Catechism of the Catholic Church* (New York, NY: Catholic Book Publishing, 1994) No. 1013

[115] Letter to the Hebrews, 9:27

Thus, Catholics believe that

> "Each man receives his eternal retribution in his immortal
> soul at the very moment of his death, in a particular
> judgment that refers his life to Christ: either entrance
> into the blessedness of heaven —through a purification or
> immediately — or immediate and everlasting dam-
> nation."[116]

In order to fully comprehend the Buddhist concept of reincarnation, however, one must also come to understand the belief in karma.

Karma is the law of moral causation, or cause and effect, which is based upon the idea that nothing happens by accident to a person. Fundamental to both Hinduism and Buddhism, there are differing views on exactly how karma works.

The Buddhist views karma as a way to explain why one person is born into luxury and another is homeless or why one man is a genius and another has severe mental challenges. According to the law of karma, none of these inequalities is accidental, but each is the result of something the person did either in this or a past life for which he or she is being punished or rewarded.

While the theory of karma is a fundamental doctrine in Buddhism, the belief is said to have been prevalent in India and Hinduism long before the advent of Buddhism. The word karma, connected to the meaning it has today, first appeared in Hindu books known as the *Upanishads,* which were composed over a wide period of time ranging from the pre-Buddhist period to the early centuries BC.

---

[116] Catechism of the Catholic Church, (Hereafter CCC), No. 1022

The concept of karma, and its resultant need for reincarnation, is incompatible with Christianity.

The Letter to the Colossians states that "When you were dead in your trespasses . . . God made you alive together with him (Christ) when he forgave us all our trespasses, erasing the record that stood against us with its legal demands. He set this aside, nailing it to the cross."[117] (2:13, 14).

In other words, our "bad karma" was nailed to the Cross of Jesus Christ, who reconciles us to the Father, so there is no need for a "redo" in another life. Instead, the Christian works out his or her salvation during this lifetime here on earth, through repentance and the Sacraments, ultimately relying on God's grace and the Savior who stands at the heart of our faith. As St. Paul teaches, "Christ Jesus came into the world to save sinners."[118]

Teacher or Savior?

But this is only the beginning of the differences between the two religions.

Christ taught that He is the "Way, the truth and the life."[119] Buddha teaches that every person must find their own path to enlightenment. In fact, his last words to his disciples were to "make of yourself a light. Rely upon yourself. Do not rely upon anyone else. Make my teachings your light. Rely upon them; do not depend upon any other teaching."[120]

---

[117] Letter to the Colossians, 2:13-14

[118] 1 Timothy, 1:15

[119] John 14:6

[120] "Catholicism and Buddhism"

Christ came into the world as the one true God who came to suffer, die, and rise again in order that we might have eternal life. Buddha is believed to be one of many *thatagata* (thus-come-one) who will come in various ages to teach that life is an illusion.

God created every person as a unique individual made in the image and likeness of Himself. Buddha teaches that individuality must perish.

Christians believe that truth, and its Author, can be known rationally; Buddhism denies existential reality and believes nothing, not even the self, can be proven to exist.

Christians believe suffering can bring us closer to God and more deeply unite us with our Suffering Lord. Buddhists believe suffering is something from which we need to escape.

These are indeed major issues of dispute, all of which stem from fundamental disparities between the two religions, particularly in the area of mysticism.

For example, there are many who say that the emphasis on detachment from the world in Buddhism is very similar to that which accompanies Christian mysticism, but this too is an erroneous interpretation.

As Pope St. John Paul II points out, in Buddhism, "to *save oneself* means, above all, to free oneself from evil by becoming *indifferent to the world, which is the source of evil.* This is the culmination of the spiritual process"[121] which is called nirvana [emphasis in original].

When the Church's spiritual masters, such as St. John of the Cross and other Carmelite mystics, speak of the need for purification and detachment from the world of the senses, the detachment is not an end

---

[121] Pope St. John Paul II, *Crossing the Threshold of Hope* (New York, NY: Alfred A. Knopf, 1994) pg. 86

in itself as it is in Buddhism. In Christian mysticism, this detachment from the world is proposed "in order to unite oneself to that which is outside of the world — by this I do not mean nirvana, but a personal God. Union with Him comes about not only through purification, but through love."[122]

St. John Paul II goes on to say that Carmelite mysticism begins at the point where the reflections of Buddha end.

The great mystical tradition of the Church, beginning with the era of the Fathers of the Eastern and Western Church, to the great theologians of Scholasticism, is not born of "a purely negative 'enlightenment'. It is not born of an awareness of the evil which exists in man's attachment to the world through the senses, the intellect and the spirit. Instead, Christian mysticism is born of the *Revelation of the living God*" [emphasis in original].[123]

Indeed, the Second Vatican Council confirmed that, unlike Buddhism and its negative attitude toward the world, Christianity in the West is marked by a positive approach to the world.

"The truth about God the Creator of the world and about Christ the Redeemer is a powerful force which inspires a positive attitude toward creation and provides a constant impetus to strive for its transformation and perfection."[124]

For the Christian, the world is God's creation. It has been redeemed by the Son and is the place where man meets God. The Buddhist, on the other hand, looks at the world through a negative lens out of a

---

[122] Ibid, pg. 87
[123] Ibid, pg. 88
[124] Ibid

conviction that it is only a source of suffering for man, a suffering from which he must break away.

As St. John Paul II concludes, the Buddhist and the Catholic have an essentially different way of perceiving the world. For this reason, he issues a strong warning to Christians who want to embrace certain ideas originating in the religious traditions of the Far East, advising them to "know one's own spiritual heritage well" before considering whether or not it should be lightly set aside.

This is because these differences play a vital role in forming the worldview of the believer, which shapes his spiritual attitude and thereby dictates the way he lives his faith.

And all of this, in turn, impacts the way he prays.

Chapter Five

Mindfulness and Christian Prayer

Several years ago, a distraught wife and mother sent an email to this writer about her husband who had taken up a twice-daily practice of mindfulness and body scan meditation for stress. One day, he decided to skip family prayer to practice mindfulness meditation instead. When she confronted him about it, saying that prayer is more restful, he disagreed and said this was not his experience, and to leave him alone.

This story is the perfect example of why St. John Paul II issued such a strong warning to Christians who want to embrace practices such as mindfulness — even for purely therapeutic purposes — which originate in the religious traditions of the Far East.

As chapter four outlined, the differences between Buddhism and Christianity are so substantial that they simply cannot be discounted when considering the adoption of even bits and pieces of eastern religious practices. And there is a perfectly logical reason for this.

The dharma created by the Buddha is a belief system with practices peculiar to his worldview, and these in turn shape the mind and the heart of the Buddhist just as Christ's Gospel teachings shape the mind and the heart of the Christian. The attitude of mind and heart that went into the formulation of the practices unique to these philosophies of life is inherent in their practices and there is always the potential of influencing the practitioner either toward or away from a particular worldview. This could be either overtly, through the encouragement of the instructor, or more subtly such as teaching the Christian to find rest not in the Spirit, but in an empty void or a strictly controlled awareness.

The above story of a man who started out practicing mindfulness to ease stress and resulted in giving up Christian prayer is just one example of how true this point has proven to be. This is not an isolated example but one that represents a common outcome among those who dabble in non-Christian eastern spiritual practices.

In other practices, such as yoga, which are also touted as being "nonspiritual" and "just exercise," studies have found that 62 percent of students and 85 percent of teachers changed their primary reason for practicing from exercise to some other reason. Even more compelling are the reasons they cite:

> "[F]or both, the top changed primary reason was spirituality. Findings suggest that most initiate yoga practice for exercise and stress relief, but for many, spirituality becomes their primary reason for maintaining the practice."[125]

---

[125] Park, C.L.; Riley, K.E.; Bedesin, E.; Stewart, V.M., "Why Practice Yoga? Practitioners Motivations for Adopting and Maintaining Yoga Practice," *Journal of Health Psychology*, June 21, 2016; 21(6):887-96

This phenomenon is only enhanced by yet another factor peculiar to Christian audiences in the West.

For the Christian, the word *meditation* means to pray. We meditate because we seek "to understand the why and how of the Christian life, in order to adhere and respond to what the Lord is asking."[126]

But in the non-Christian East, meditation is a purely mental exercise, a way to manage thoughts and/or to induce an altered state of consciousness where one can achieve personal enlightenment and self-discovery.

Although these differences could not be clearer, they are a source of great confusion in the West simply because too many Christians are unaware of them. They tend to be poorly catechized in their own faith as well as in the eastern religions that are being popularized in the West; and because of this, the two forms of meditation are easily conflated.

In other words, whether it's intended to be prayer or not, eastern practices very often work their way into the prayer life of the Christian who engages with them.

This is also true of mindfulness. Even though it is not prayer, we know from chapter four that it readily overlaps with spirituality. This may not be true with the minimal exercise described in chapter one, which is nothing more than a focused awareness on the present moment, but the mindfulness that is growing in popularity today in the West is almost exclusively practiced as a meditation technique. For example, Breathing Space Meditation, Body Scan Meditation, Movement Meditation, et cetera, are all techniques which originate in the practice of Buddhism.

---

[126] CCC, No. 2705

But even among those Christians who are aware of the differences between the two types of meditation, many are prone to incorporating eastern methods into their prayer life due to erroneous interpretations of the Vatican II document, *Nostra Aetate*, the *Declaration on the Relationship of the Church to Non-Christian Religions.* This document says that we are permitted to adopt what is good from other religions. It teaches that "The Catholic Church rejects nothing that is true and holy in these religions" because it believes that other religions "often reflect a ray of that Truth which enlightens all men"[127] What is often ignored is that a reflection of a ray is not truth that is *directly from* the source but only a *reflection* of the source that is found in the Catholic faith.

Unfortunately, too many Christians are unaware of the fact that a very important clarification of this teaching — as it applies to prayer —

was given by Cardinal Joseph Ratzinger in a later document entitled, *A Letter to the Bishops on Some Aspects of Christian Meditation.*

In this document, Ratzinger teaches that when it comes to prayer, we can adopt what is good from other religions, "so long as the Christian conception of prayer, its logic and requirements are never obscured."[128]

Herein lies the problem. Buddhist and/or Hindu meditation techniques, by their very nature, are diametrically opposed to the Christian conception of prayer, which is "the raising of one's heart and mind to God."[129]

Hence the warning by Cardinal Jean-Louis Tauran, president of the

---

[127] Nostra Aetate, Declaration on the Revelation of the Church to Non-Christian Religions, Pope Paul VI, October 28, 1965, No. 2

[128] Congregation for the Doctrine of the Faith, *Letter to the Bishops of the Catholic Church on Some Aspects of Christian Meditation,* 1989, No. 16

[129] CCC, No. 2559

Pontifical Council for Interreligious Dialogue that the poorly-catechized Christian should not take part in any kind of interreligious dialogue.

> Christians, often ignorant of the content of their own
> faith and incapable because of this of living of and for it,
> are not capable of interreligious dialogue that always
> begins with the assertion of one's own convictions. There
> is no room for syncretism or relativism! Faced with
> adepts from other religions with a strong religious
> identity, it is necessary to present motivated and
> doctrinally equipped Christians.[130]

Neglecting to heed this advice has created the perfect storm that has enabled eastern beliefs to infiltrate western spirituality in seemingly innocent ways, such as the promotion of mindfulness as a "psychological tool," yoga as "just exercise", and transcendental meditation as a "relaxation exercise." For the majority of today's marginally catechized Christians, for whom meditation is synonymous with prayer, when eastern practices involving mind-blanking or mindfulness are introduced to them, they are naturally inclined to incorporate these practices into Christian prayer whether appropriate or not, with many believing that this is actually permissible.

All of the above reasons are why the mindfulness techniques being promoted today are problematic for the Christian. Regardless of how neatly the "lines" are drawn on paper, in real life, those lines are easily blurred.

---

[130] Thirteenth Ordinary General Assembly of the Synod of Bishops, October, 2012

"Catholic Mindfulness?"

The following is an example of how easily those lines can be blurred.

A recently developed Catholic mindfulness program introduces students to the practice of mindfulness as a psychological exercise that is to be practiced *before daily prayer*. However, in one of the exercises, the instructor tells his students, "Start by gently calling to mind the presence of God and recall the words of St. Paul to glorify God with your bodies."[131]

Students are then led in a guided eastern meditation exercise known as Mindful Movement, which focuses on awareness of the breath and various stretching movements.

"See this exercise as a chance to cultivate awareness of the body and even the smallest movement . . . As you're standing, notice the contact between your feet and the floor. . . On the next inbreath, slowly and mindfully raise your arms out to the sides . . . Breath by breath, really tune into the changing sensations as your arms move, perhaps feeling the clothes moving on the surface of your skin . . ."[132]

The exercise ends with another prayer to God.

Even though he insists that mindfulness is not prayer, and that the exercise should be practiced *before* prayer, the instructor begins with a prayer! It invokes God and cites a scripture that suggests God will be glorified in the exercise. Of course we want God to be glorified in everything we do, even mental or physical exercise, but anyone introducing an eastern practice such as mindfulness to the general public

---

[131] Bottaro, Dr. Gregory, "Catholic Mindfulness," Lesson Three, accessed online
[132] Ibid

should be more aware of the serious pastoral issues surrounding the Christian conception of meditation as outlined above. Otherwise, for the average Christian, in whose mind eastern meditation techniques and western prayer are already muddled, this exercise easily slips into the realm of prayer regardless of the intent of the instructor.

It is imperative that Christians understand the critical differences between eastern and Christian meditation, all of which are shaped by their underlying belief systems, so that they can more readily appreciate why dabbling in non-Christian meditation techniques could pose spiritual dangers.

Let us begin with the most obvious difference, which is between the God of the West and the "gods" of the East. In Christianity,

> "The holy, Catholic, apostolic Roman Church believes and professes that there is one true, living God, the Creator and Lord of heaven and earth. He is almighty, eternal, beyond measure, incomprehensible, and infinite in intellect, will and in every perfection. Since He is one unique spiritual substance, entirely simple and unchangeable, He must be declared really and essentially distinct from the world, perfectly happy in Himself and by his very nature, and inexpressibly exalted over all things that exist or can be conceived other than Himself."[133]

This is starkly different from the gods of eastern mysticism which range from being too numerous to count to being nonexistent

---

[133] Hardon, Fr. John A., *The Catholic Encyclopedia* (New York, NY: *Doubleday Religious Publishing*, 2013) pg. 192, citing Denzinger 3001.

(Buddhism) and/or based on a pantheistic belief in Brahman, who is described as a "totally impersonal, infinite energy" (Hindu).[134]

Naturally, this presence — or absence — of God impacts every aspect of the meditation practices of the Christian and the non-Christian.

The most apparent difference is in the focus of the meditation. For the Christian, the focus is on God. The prayer seeks to understand the why and how of the Christian life, in order to adhere and respond to what the Lord is asking.

But for the Buddhist, the focus is on the self. The aim is to achieve self-enlightenment, with the eventual goal of achieving "nirvana," the state in which one extinguishes belief in the self and ceases to exist.

In the practice of mindfulness meditation, the practitioner is entirely focused on the self — whether it be the body and its sensations, the ebb and flow of its breath, or the movement of its limbs — and to not be judgmental about any thought or feeling.

Christian meditation, on the other hand, is a double orientation which involves "introspection but is essentially also a meeting with God. Far from being a merely human effort, Christian mysticism is essentially a dialogue which 'implies an attitude of conversion, a flight from 'self' to the 'you' of God.'"[135]

The Buddhist nonbelief in the soul is another glaring discrepancy between the two schools of prayer. This is in stark contrast to Christian prayer which is sourced in the Spirit who inhabits the soul and who

---

[134] Sculley, Max, D.L.S., *Yoga, Tai Chi, Reiki: A Guide for Christians* (Ballan, Australia: Modotti Press, 2012) pg. 29
[135] Ibid

"comes to the aid of our weakness; for we do not know how to pray as we ought, but the Spirit itself intercedes with inexpressible groanings."[136]

Even the much-touted moment-by-moment awareness encouraged in mindfulness meditation is incompatible with the awareness which is called for in Christian prayer.

Father Thomas Dubay explains:

> Hence, it follows . . . that a Buddhist awareness produced
> by human techniques and methods is radically different
> from our theistic contemplation. Our communion with
> the living God is completely interpersonal, intensely so:
> we adore, love, praise, thirst for our triune Beloved. . . ..
> What the Buddhist describes is entirely impersonal, not
> at all a relationship between persons, let alone an
> intimate one.[137]

Another serious discrepancy is found in the aim of Buddhist meditation, which is to extinguish belief in the self and cease to exist. This is very different from the Christian who aims to die to self, not by ceasing to exist but by casting off the "old self"[138] and putting on the new self.[139]

"This is the 'life' we must lose, this the 'self' we must abandon if we are to have true life and become that self God wants us to be, which only

---

[136] Romans 8:26

[137] Dubay, Father Thomas, S.M., *Prayer Primer: Igniting a Fire Within* (San Francisco, CA: *Ignatius Press*, 2002) pg. 153

[138] Romans 6:6

[139] Colossians 3:10

God can know and ultimately only God can bring into being."[140]

Many eastern mystics claim that divine realities such as these are beyond words, thought and personality and that the only way to find this kind of "enlightenment" is to extinguish one's critical capacities.

However, the Bible never calls us to do this. "Do not conform yourselves to this age but be transformed by the renewal of your mind, that you may discern what is the will of God, what is good and pleasing and perfect."[141]The last thing the Christian wants to do is shut down their mind or senses. Instead, whether prayer is expressed in words or gestures, "it is the whole man who prays."[142] In other words, Christian meditation "engages thought, imagination, emotion, and desire" in prayer.[143]

In more advanced forms of infused contemplation, when the Lord chooses to suspend the faculties, even this is done with the full awareness and consent of the prayer.

"The soul is often absorbed, or, to put it better, the Lord absorbs it in Himself, suspending all the faculties for a while," explains St. Teresa of Avila. Although this suspension is brief, "since the loving impulse and elevation of the spirit was great, the will remains absorbed"[144] because the will of the person has become one with the will of his God.

---

[140] Burrows, Ruth OCD, *Essence of Prayer*, (Mahwah, NJ: *HiddenSpring*, 2006) pg. 3

[141] Romans 12:2

[142] CCC, No. 2562

[143] CCC, No. 2708

[144] Avila, St. Teresa, *The Collected Works of St. Teresa of Avila*, Volume I, *Book of Her Life*, Chapter 20 (Washington, DC: ICS Publications) pg. 180

Giving Up Control

This leads us to yet another essential incongruity between mindfulness meditation and Christian prayer. In mindfulness, the practitioner spends his time in meditation attempting to control his or her awareness, trying to maintain it upon either a single point, the rhythm of his breathing, or whatever is most prominent in his consciousness. Even to remain nonjudgmental toward any thoughts and impulses that come to mind requires effort. In other words, maintaining control is the key to this practice.

But in Christian meditation, the exact opposite is true. As one's commitment to the Gospel and trust in God deepens, the Christian gradually and willingly relinquishes control of one's prayer life to the Almighty, which is essential to growth in prayer and intimacy with God.

This is precisely what is taught by Teresa of Avila, who describes four distinct stages of prayer that the faithful Christian may experience in the course of one's lifetime. Beginning with vocal prayer and advancing into mental prayer and meditation, if God so chooses, this is followed by infused contemplation which culminates in transforming union with God. The modus operandi of this progression is to gradually relinquish control of our prayer life to God. In this process, we die to self in order to live more fully in Christ, thereby giving up control of our interior life through an ever more complete surrender to God's will.

"Learning true prayer means learning to die in the sense Jesus meant by this: dying to egotism, self-determination and self-achieving, and letting God recreate us in love in a way that only God can do."[145]

---

[145] Essence of Prayer, pg. 7

Even the Buddhist idea of focusing entirely on the present moment in meditation can be stifling to the Christian who is taught to focus on remembering God's work in the past. "I will recall the deeds of the Lord; yes, recall your wonders of old."[146] Equally important are numerous passages in Scripture which teach the follower of Christ to live with an eternal perspective. "I long to depart this life and be with Christ [for] that is far better."[147]

In other words, the Christian is meant to see the present in its full context — with the past and the future fully present in each moment.

The Body and the Emotions

These differences in focus between the two schools of meditation also manifest in another problematic area, that of the psychophysical symbolism present in eastern meditation, such as the focus on breathing in the mindfulness practice known as Breathing Space meditation. While the Christian has a close equivalent in the "Jesus Prayer," which consists of repeating a short prayer along with the natural rhythm of breathing, spiritual masters from both East and West agree that not everyone is suited to making use of this symbolism, since not everybody is able to pass from the material sign to the spiritual reality that is being sought.

Cardinal Ratzinger explains:

Understood in an inadequate and incorrect way, the

---

[146] Psalm 77:12

[147] Philippians 1:23

symbolism can even become an idol and thus an obstacle to the raising up of the spirit to God. To live out in one's prayer the full awareness of one's body as a symbol is even more difficult: it can degenerate into a cult of the body and can lead surreptitiously to considering all bodily sensations as spiritual experiences.[148]

The Christian who has not yet moved beyond the early stages of prayer and who is still being guided largely by the senses rather than faith is particularly vulnerable to this error. This is because eastern forms of meditation, either of mind-managing or keen awareness exercises, create pleasant bodily sensations which they too often equate with "good" spiritual experiences that the beginner still finds so irresistible.

This may well have been the case with the example given at the beginning of this chapter. Notice how the man began his practice of mindfulness to better handle stress. At some point during his practice, it became associated in his mind with prayer. And because he was still coming to prayer for his own benefit, when Christian prayer was not as "restful" for him anymore, it was an easy switch to turn to mindfulness meditation to satisfy those desires.

The poorly catechized Christian who is unaware of the Christian mystical tradition doesn't know that he is expected to eventually progress beyond the more self-centered reasons for prayer that motivated him at the beginning of his spiritual life. He is not aware that he must eventually learn how to come to prayer for God's sake, and not just his own.

---

[148] *Some Aspects of Christian Meditation*, No. 27

In fact, this progression is considered to be a crucial step in spiritual maturity, and one that normally comes from acceptance of the "dark night" experiences that are common for Christians who take a serious interest in their interior life. For example, experiences of sudden dryness in prayer (those which are not associated with laxity or clinging to sin-habits), are one of the most common ways that the Lord teaches the soul to begin to come to Him in prayer regardless of how "good" or "bad" is the prayer experience. Too many Christians are not adequately instructed in the fundamentals of the spiritual life and, when tested, either turn back and cease praying altogether or find themselves drawn into more self-gratifying eastern or New Age meditation techniques.

The altering of consciousness in mindfulness is another "feel good" quality associated with eastern meditation techniques that can easily lure the Christian. The aim to achieve a "higher" or "altered" state of consciousness in mindfulness, such as in the Expanding Awareness Meditation technique described in chapter one, is to suspend rational patterns of thought so as to better grasp sacred realities.

Moira Noonan, author of *Spiritual Deceptions in the Church and the Culture*, was once involved in vipassana meditation, which many reference as the forerunner of today's popular mindfulness movement. She describes:

> We were led through the process by the master —
> completely silent — completely going into a place of
> blankness, of emptiness, of nothingness — a place of
> liberation to feel completely free of any attachment to
> self, desire, emotion, thoughts to get to the place where

we don't exist.[149]

Naturally, when we put aside all thoughts, including those that are distressing, and enter into an altered state of consciousness where we are totally detached from the world and our problems and even ourselves, we will experience a kind of temporary bliss. But these experiences are not without serious risk to the practitioner. Being in an altered state leaves us vulnerable to spiritual influences the same way that we're vulnerable to suggestion while in a hypnotic trance. A person's will is suspended during an altered state, leaving them unable to defend themselves.

The Pontifical document, *Jesus Christ the Bearer of the Water of Life,* warns that these states "create an atmosphere of psychic weakness (and vulnerability)." [150]

In their 1994 book, *A Catholic Response to the New Age Phenomena*, the Irish Theological Commission elaborates further by saying that in these altered states "people are open to spirit influences without being in control, for they have surrendered to this 'consciousness'."[151]

Nowhere in Scripture are we taught that an altered state of consciousness is necessary to commune with God.

Mindfulness and Recollection

In spite of these serious differences, many Christian still believe that

---

[149] Phone interview

[150] Section 4

[151] Irish Theological Commission, *A Catholic Response to the New Age Phenomenon* (Dublin, Ireland: *Veritas Publications,* 1994) cited in *The Learn to Discern Compendium* (Oldsmar, Florida: Simon Peter Press, 2015) pg.223

they can adopt bits and pieces of mindfulness techniques in order to enhance their own prayer experience. One of the most prevalent examples is the belief that mindfulness can help one to recollect themselves for prayer. But even this more limited use has serious drawbacks.

As Cardinal Ratzinger explains, Christians don't need techniques to recollect themselves. They need faith, and grace.

> Without doubt, a Christian needs certain periods of
> retreat into solitude to be recollected and, in God's
> presence, rediscover his path. Nevertheless, given his
> character as a creature, and as a creature who knows that
> only in grace is he secure, his method of getting closer to
> God is not based on any technique in the strict sense of
> the word. That would contradict the spirit of childhood
> called for by the Gospel. Genuine Christian mysticism has
> nothing to do with technique: it is always a gift of God,
> and the one who benefits from it knows himself to be
> unworthy.[152]

In other words, even for the limited purpose of providing recollection, mindfulness can undermine the spirit of Christian prayer. This is primarily because, as we learned earlier in this chapter, the focus of mindfulness is on the self rather than on finding oneself in God, and these two intentions are essentially incompatible.

> Thus, Christian prayer is at the same time always
> authentically personal and communitarian. It flees from

---

[152] *Letter to the Bishops on Some Aspects of Christian Meditation,* No. 23

impersonal techniques or from concentrating on oneself,
which can create kind of rut, imprisoning the person
praying in a spiritual privatism which is incapable of a
free openness to the transcendental God.[153]

Christians do not need Buddhist techniques to recollect themselves. Instead, we do recollect ourselves by retreating into solitude and silence. But here we are not only talking about the kind of silence defined by St. Benedict as *quies* — which is the absence of noise, a quiet, physical silence. We are also referring to *silentium*, which is a silencing of the heart, the quieting of the passions and inordinate attachments that clutter the soul. As Cardinal Robert Sarah describes, it results "from the absence of disordered affections or excessive desires" and is "above all the positive attitude of someone who prepares to welcome God by listening."[154]

This quieting of the soul is something that the Christians are drawn into by God as they yield to an ever-deepening commitment to the agape love of the Gospel, which results in the kind of selflessness that can only be acquired by the gradual dying to self and yielding to God.

Even in the limited use of recollecting ourselves for prayer, the practice of mindfulness with its fixation on the self falls woefully short of the kind of recollection needed in order to enjoy the full Christian experience of the Living God.

Others practitioners believe mindfulness tactics can be used by both Buddhists and Christians to promote self-discovery, but this too is an

---

[153] Ibid, No. 3
[154] Sarah, Cardinal Robert, "Silence in the Liturgy," *L'Osservatore Romano,* January 30, 2016

erroneous supposition based on a faulty understanding of the concept in both Buddhism and Christianity.

The reason why the Christian focus in prayer is always on the "Other", Who is God, is because it is only in Him that we discover who we truly are. No amount of awareness of our body or breath or movement can reveal ourselves as acutely as the self-knowledge that comes to us as a gift of the Spirit.

Writes St. Teresa of Avila:

> In my opinion we shall never completely know ourselves
> if we don't strive to know God. By gazing at His
> grandeur, we get in touch with our own lowliness; by
> looking at Hs purity we shall see our own filth; by
> pondering His humility we shall see how far we are from
> being humble.[155]

And because we are seeing ourselves in God, these revelations do not make us fearful or ashamed; rather they fill us with love for this God who upholds us in spite of ourselves and showers us with mercy. Thus, true Godward self-knowledge inspires confidence in God and distrust in self, what the great spiritual master J. P. de Caussade called "the two great props of the spiritual life."[156]

Instead of sitting in the tightly controlled self-awareness of mindfulness, one can focus on God and experience not only the

---

[155] Avila, St. Teresa, *The Interior Castle, Collected Works,* Volume II (Washington, DC: ICS Publications, 1980, pg. 292

[156] de Caussade, Father J. P., S.J., *Letters of Father De Caussade on the Practice of Self-Abandonment* (Rockford, Illinois: Tan Books and Publishes, Inc., 1987) pg. 243

recollection they seek, but a kind of self-discovery that is accompanied by dynamic spiritual growth and empowerment.

The radical differences between eastern and western meditation cannot be overstated. This, coupled with the prevailing confusion among the Christian population about these differences, what is permissible to adopt, and how eastern techniques can actually impede our spiritual growth beyond "feel good" religion into the realms of a closer union with God, should either dissuade any Christian from, or at the very least inspire a grave sense of caution to any Christian wishing to, dabble in these areas.

But what about those who are seeking a way to better control their thoughts, both inside and outside of prayer? Is there a Christian alternative to mindfulness?

Chapter Six

Christian Alternatives to Mindfulness

The last chapter made it quite clear that mindfulness has no place in Christian prayer, either as a prelude, component, or adjunct.

But that doesn't mean it's easy to resist. Mindfulness has become the latest fad, and all fads are accompanied by a certain amount of pressure for the individual to conform in order to be reap the social benefits of those who tend to follow fads. And fads are usually very profitable for those who promote them, which explains why mindfulness is surrounded by more hype than fact.

However, even those Christians who are not swayed by the social pressures of fad-following may find themselves compelled to practice mindfulness by medical professionals or psychologists, some of whom insist that it is needed in order to deal effectively with their anxiety. These providers frequently cite studies filled with impressive findings, or tout research that found that the practice of mindfulness can actually alter the brain and reduce the symptoms of anxiety.

There is no need to submit to this pressure because, as we learned in chapter three, many of the studies done so far are methodologically challenged, and there is plenty of research that resulted in negative outcomes for patients.

In fact, in the course of my writing this book, yet another study was released where researchers found that Buddhist-derived meditation techniques, such as those used in the practice of mindfulness, were producing unpleasant and even distressing experiences in people. These experiences ranged from sensitivity to light to anxiety, panic, insomnia, involuntary movement, and dizziness. It also found that some of the effects of meditation that felt positive while in a retreat setting became burdensome outside of this venue and even interfered with their work function.[157]

Responsible healthcare providers should provide all of this information to patients to enable them to make fully informed decisions about whether or not to participate in mindfulness.

Altering the Brain

Even the claim that mindfulness alters the brain can be challenged. According to a new field of study known as neurotheology, *all* forms of meditation can alter the brain, not just mindfulness.

Neurotheology is drawing prominent researchers from across the U.S. and Canada, who have found that the brains of people who spend time in prayer and meditation are different from those who don't engage

---

[157] Lindahl, Jared R.; Fisher, Nathan E.; Cooper, David J.; Rosen, Rochelle K.; Britton, Willoughby B.; "The varieties of contemplative experience: A mixed-methods study of meditation-related challenges in Western Buddhists," *PLOS Journal*, May 24, 2017

in these practices.

One of the most notable of these researchers is Andrew Newberg, a neuroscientist at the University of Pennsylvania, who has been scanning the brains of religious people for more than a decade. Newberg has found that people who meditate, from Franciscan nuns to Tibetan Buddhists, go dark in the parietal lobe — the area of the brain that is related to sensory information and helps us to form our sense of self. He also found some areas of increased activity in the frontal lobes, which handle focused attention, in a person who was praying intently while being subjected to a SPECT [single-photon emission computerized tomography] scan.[158]

"The more you focus on something — whether that's math or auto racing or football or God — the more that becomes your reality, the more it becomes written into the neural connections of your brain," Newberg says.

Neuroscientist Richard Davidson agrees. He has found that anyone can change their brain with experience and training.

"You can sculpt your brain just as you'd sculpt your muscles if you went to the gym," he says. "Our brains are continuously being sculpted, whether you like it or not, wittingly or unwittingly."[159]

---

[158] Haggarty, Barbara Bradley, NPR, "Prayer May Reshape Your Brain – and Your Reality," May 20, 2009
[159] Ibid

Psychological or Spiritual?

Another argument in favor of mindfulness, especially attractive to those Christians who are wary of dabbling in non-Christian practices, is that mindfulness is a psychological practice and not a spiritual one.

But this statement also finds itself at odds with the facts, such as those found in a recent research paper which questions why therapists are so willing to ignore the spiritual component of mindfulness when these very same aspects could be beneficial for patients.

> In the process of establishing a reputation for scientific rigor, however, many within the mindfulness movement have been keen to distance themselves from the religious roots of mindfulness in the Buddhist tradition. This paper looks at these roots, examining the Satipatthana Sutta, the key text on mindfulness in the Buddhist canon. It reconsiders the practice's origins as a spiritual vehicle . . .[160]

The researchers find that in the modern age, secularism has in many ways replaced religion as the prevailing ethos and value system, and this influence has found "fertile ground" in the therapy world.

"In the functional arena of mental health provision, what arose as a spiritual practice has been repackaged and presented as a system of psychological exploration, devoid of some of the original associations which it bore in the spiritual arena."

---

[160] Brazier, Caroline, "Roots of Mindfulness," *European Journal of Counseling and Psychotherapy*, May, 2013

Regardless of how therapists may want to distance themselves from the spiritual roots of mindfulness, this doesn't change the fact that it is, in essence, a spiritual practice. Remember, as we described in chapter two, Kabat-Zinn went to great lengths to incorporate the dharma of Buddhism into the scientific practice of mindfulness but in a way that kept it hidden from those who would not accept these spiritual connections. He admitted to deliberately using the umbrella term of mindfulness as a kind of "place-holder for the entire dharma . . . as a potentially skillful means for bringing the streams of alive, embodied dharma understanding and of clinical medicine together."[161]

Because *dharma* is defined as "the teaching or religion of the Buddha," and one of the definitions of *spiritual* is "relating to religion or religious belief,"[162] it's safe to say that mindfulness is indeed spiritual.

Relieving Anxiety

However, the most prevalent reason given for taking up the practice of mindfulness is how effectively it can help us control our focus and keep us from ruminating on things that can upset us or cause anxiety.

Perhaps this argument is the most compelling because it's the most common. The desire to control our wandering minds is hardly a new one. Better known as "thought control," it's the undisputed darling of the New Age and manifests itself today in a variety of methods. Some are adopted from the meditation practices of the ancients while others originate in the nineteenth century's New Thought movement.

---

[161] Kabat-Zinn, Jon, "Some Reflections on the Origins of MBSR, Skillful Means, and the Trouble with Maps," *Contemporary Buddhism*, Vol. 12, No. 1, May, 2011
[162] Oxford Dictionary

Mindfulness is simply the latest version, coming into vogue along with its demands to purposely focus on the present moment "as if your life depended on it."[163] It utilizes Buddhist-based meditation techniques in its practice — much like Centering Prayer, with its rigid thought management exercises, borrows from transcendental meditation.

Non-prayer-based forms of thought control are also quite prevalent. One example is *A Course in Miracles,* which is a year-long study that retrains the mind to form a different perception of the world, preferably one that is not based on Judeo-Christian values.

Popular self-help books are also very much in the business of selling thought control, such as *The Secret* and *The Law of Attraction,* which teach readers how to use their minds to attract good fortune and well-being.

Landmark and other motivational training seminars aim at accomplishing the same thing — change the way we think in order to achieve success.

And because most of us, Christians included, suffer from destructive thought patterns to some extent or another, we could all use some help in this area.

But that help needn't come in the form of New Age or other non-Christian methods because we have our own methods for thought control, and they come straight from Scripture.

> [W]hatever is true, whatever is honorable, whatever is
> just, whatever is pure, whatever is lovely, whatever is
> gracious, if there is any excellence and if there is anything

---

[163] Kabat-Zinn, Jon, *Mindfulness for Beginners* (Boulder, Colorado: Sounds True, 2012) pg. 17

worthy of praise, think about these things. . . .. Then the
God of peace will be with you.[164]

When it comes to controlling the mind, and directing our focus,
Jesus Christ is the only sure guide. First, because He has the power to
heal us of whatever is causing negative thoughts or other anxiety-
causing ruminations of the mind, such as a poor self-image. Second,
because the mind is a well-known spiritual battleground, and the
inability to focus is just one of many ploys used by Satan to oppress the
faithful, Jesus is our only means to uncover and then defeat this
diabolical cause. Third, because Jesus Himself calls us to exercise this
kind of control, we can count on His grace to enable us to do so. This is
far better than having to rely on our own weak and often inconsistent
efforts as would be the case when practicing mindfulness.

The Christian is called to put on "the mind of Christ"[165] and in order
to do that, we must "take captive every thought to make it obedient to
Christ."[166]

In his booklet, *Thought Control: Architect of Character*, Fr. John H.
Hampsch, CMF, tells us that we "take captive every thought" by being
vigilant over what we let into our minds.

> Erroneous input into a computer results in erroneous
> output. So it is with our minds. If we fill them with the
> garbage of sleazy literature or questionable television
> programs or films, with worldly conversation or thoughts
> of envy, jealousy, avarice, pride, morbid fear, resentment,

---

[164] Philippians 4:8-9

[165] 1 Corinthians 2:16

[166] 2 Corinthians 10:5

etc. then we leave little or no room for God to work in us.[167]

The first thing we need to do is learn how to instantly drop unwanted thoughts. Negative thoughts — what some describe as "rogue" thoughts — must be dismissed the minute we notice them, without stopping to acknowledge them or consider them in any way, which only serves to reinforce them.

This is precisely what the spiritual masters teach those who are striving to achieve peace of soul.

> In the first place, take care never to harbor voluntarily in your heart any thought calculated to grieve, disquiet, or dishearten it. From one point of view, such thoughts are more dangerous than impure temptations. Your need then, is to allow them to pass you by, despising them and letting them fall like a stone into the sea. You must resist them by concentrating your attention upon contrary reflections . . .[168]

For example, if you find yourself ruminating about seeking revenge for some injustice done to you, as soon as you become aware of these thoughts, reject them in Jesus name, and replace them with a prayer for whoever or whatever was responsible for treating you unfairly. This not only returns your peace of soul, but can be the start of a healing process

---

[167] Hampsch, Father John H., CMF, *Thought Control: Architect of Character* (Goleta, CA: Queenship Publishing Co., 2000)

[168] de Caussade, Father J. P., S.J., *Letters of Father de Caussade on the Practice of Self-Abandonment* (Rockford, Illinois: Tan Books and Publishers, Inc. 1987) pg. 204

that will open your soul to a flood of new grace.

As this suggestion illustrates, God's method of thought control is much more expansive than simply keeping your focus on the present moment.

However, there are some promoters of Christian mindfulness who suggest that Christianity might somehow be the key to mindfulness, and that it can actually lead to that non-judgmental focus on the present moment that is mindfulness. A closer look at this suggestion reveals that Christianity is not the *key* to mindfulness, it's the *replacement*.

This replacement comes in the form of two beloved Christian practices, the Sacrament of the Present Moment and the Practice of the Presence of God.

Sacrament of the Present Moment

The Sacrament of the Present Moment is a spiritual path outlined by one of the greatest spiritual directors in the history of the Church, Father J. P. de Caussade, S.J.

On this path, we learn that Christ comes to us in a new and living way every day, and in every moment of every day. For this reason, our attention must remain focused on all of the events that occur, minute-by-minute, from the trivial to the sublime, because this is how God speaks to us.

This was the spirituality of the Blessed Virgin Mary and St. Joseph, who did not have access to spiritual directors, the guidance of hagiography, or volumes of theology.

> All their attention was focused on the present, minute by minute; like the hand of a clock that marks the minutes of

each hour covering the distance along which it has to travel. Constantly prompted by divine impulsion, they found themselves imperceptibly turned toward the next task that God had ready for them at each hour of the day.[169]

Their lives were guided by a pure and simple commitment to the will of God in whatever form it might present itself in each moment of the day. Even though, on the surface, Mary and Joseph were just ordinary people living an ordinary life in the village of Nazareth, we know that beneath this commonplace exterior, they were unparalleled in holiness. These heights of sanctity were acquired through a complete reliance on God's grace and obedience to His Will in whatever way it chose to manifest in the everyday moments of their lives.

But what is the secret of how to find this treasure — this minute grain of mustard seed? There is none. It is available to us always, everywhere. Like God, every creature, whether friend or foe, pours it out generously, making it flow through every part of our bodies and souls to the very center of our being. Divine action cleanses the universe, pervading and flowing over all creatures. Wherever they are it pursues them. It precedes them, accompanies them, follows them. We have only to allow ourselves to be borne along on its tide.[170]

---

[169] de Caussade, Father J. P., S.J., *The Sacrament of the Present Moment* (New York, NY: Harper One), pg. 1
[170] Ibid, pg. 3

Those who abandon themselves to this way of life and who live to discover God's will in the everyday moments of their life do so without the need to question, to judge, to consider the consequences or the causes or the reasons why this or that may happen.

Instead, "we leave God to act in everything, reserving for ourselves only love and obedience to the present moment."[171]

And by doing so, God becomes the source of life for these souls, not through ideas or enlightenment or reasoning, but hidden in the operation and truth of his grace as it manifests in each moment of every day of our lives.

> And so God and his divine order must be cherished in all
> things, just as it is, without asking for anything more;
> whatever he may offer us is not our business but God's,
> and what he ordains is best. How simple is this perfect
> and total surrender of self to the world of God! And
> there, in continual self-forgetfulness to be forever
> occupied in loving and obeying him, untroubled by all
> those doubts and perplexities, reverses and anxieties
> which attend the hope of his salvation and true
> perfection![172]

This brief expose of the Sacrament of the Present Moment should be enough to expose the similarities — and the immense differences —

between this devotion and the practice of mindfulness. About the only thing the two practices have in common is that they both call for a non-

---

[171] Ibid, pg. 11
[172] Ibid, pg. 25

judgmental focus on the now, but the underlying motives and end of this focus could not be further apart.

In mindfulness, one focuses on the present moment to become aware of it, to escape the *doing* mode and enter into the *being* mode in order to awaken to the experience of each moment.

In the Sacrament of the Present Moment, we dwell in the present not to enter into a state of awareness but into a state of abandonment to the will of God. These are two entirely different aims. One is focused on what *we're* doing in the present moment and the other is focused on what *He's* doing in the present moment. Instead of being about moment-to-moment awareness, it's about moment-to-moment surrender. Put simply, the Christian remains in the present moment not for the sake of the present moment, but for the sake of hearing the voice of the God who speaks to it in that moment.

Some proponents of the Christian use of mindfulness say that the explicit understanding of the psychological process for paying attention to the present moment hasn't been developed much in Christianity because it's more of a psychological than a spiritual process. For this reason, Christianity hasn't been concerned with the "how" of achieving this attention to the present moment. Mindfulness then, can be seen as the "secret" to staying in the present.

However, as de Caussade writes, "But what is the secret of how to find this treasure — this minute grain of mustard seed? There is none. It is available to us always, everywhere."

Some say they use mindfulness as a way to focus or "center" themselves before turning their focus to God, but this raises the question — why bother? If we're going to exert all that effort on focusing — and mindfulness does require a great deal of effort — why waste time and energy focusing on a superfluous "side trip" when we could just skip that and invest our energy on going straight to God? Even though it's true that both practices require effort, one practice is fueled by Divine grace while the other is fueled by our own weak human efforts. Which one is more likely to succeed?

This argument becomes even stronger when we consider the companion practice to the Sacrament of the Present Moment, one in which we learn the most compelling reason of all to remain focused on the present.

The Practice of the Presence of God

The practice of the presence of God is derived from the writings of Brother Lawrence of the Resurrection, a Discalced Carmelite brother who lived at a monastery in Paris during the seventeenth century. He was a simple man who considered himself to be clumsy and inept and deserving of no higher work than making soup in the kitchen of the monastery. And yet it was to this humble man that God revealed the secrets of His Kingdom here on earth, secrets revealed to us in a small collection of letters written three hundred years ago, which became one of the Church's most beloved classics, *The Practice of the Presence of God*.

As Brother Lawrence explains,

> The holiest and most necessary practice in the spiritual
> life is that of the presence of God. It consists in taking
> delight in and becoming accustomed to his divine
> company, speaking humbly and conversing lovingly with
> him all the time, at every moment, without rule or
> measures; especially in times of temptation, suffering,

aridity, weariness, even infidelity and sin.[173]

It is "an application of our mind to God, or a remembrance of God present, that can be brought about by either the imagination or the understanding."[174]

Of course, this doesn't mean that we spend our whole day paying attention to God and nothing else. Rather, he describes this as a "simple attentiveness and a general loving awareness of God" that is more like a quiet and secret conversation of the soul with God. We train ourselves to be continually aware of His presence within us, and we strive to live constantly in that awareness, even though it is usually something that lingers only at the back of our mind, like background music playing in the lobby of our lives.

St. Teresa of Avila once described this awareness as being akin to standing in a room full of people when suddenly the lights go out. Even though we no longer see the other people, we are nevertheless fully aware that they are still in the room with us.

However, one is encouraged to go beyond this general awareness to a more particular form by "checking in" with the Lord more formally throughout the day, either through short ejaculations such as "Lord, be with me" or "Help me in this endeavor, Lord." This can also be accomplished by nothing more than a simple glance within, to the place where God dwells within us by grace, to acknowledge him, love him, adore him, praise him — whatever the heart moves us to do.

---

[173] Brother Lawrence of the Resurrection, OCD, *Writings and Conversations on the Practice of the Presence of God*, translated by Salvatore Sciurba, OCD (Washington, DC: ICS Publications, 2015) Spiritual Maxim No. 6, pg. 38

[174] Ibid, Spiritual Maxim No. 20, pg. 42

Just like any other method of thought control, this practice requires discipline, especially faithfulness to prayer and meditation on the Word of God, which gradually cultivates within us a knowledge and love for God. As St. John of the Cross writes, in time, the faithful soul will gradually acquire a habitual general loving knowledge of God that is "neither distinct nor particular" but is rather an act of "general, loving, peaceful and tranquil knowledge, drinking wisdom and love and delight."[175]

This gentle awareness, which exudes from the center of our soul, gradually becomes second nature. It becomes a kind of wordless sharing of everything we encounter throughout the day; an intriguing email, a moment of laughter, even a long wait in line at the supermarket. Realizing His Presence slowly starts to become a habit, and eventually a way of life. Regardless of what we're doing — working, resting, eating, sleeping — we feel "accompanied" by a powerful and yet loving Presence which in turn fosters a deep and abiding sense of security.

This practice is especially comforting when confronting stressful moments in life. As Brother Lawrence describes, in these moments, he would simply call on his Friend and say, "I'm capable of nothing without you," and God's help would be there in an instant — and usually in much greater proportions than he would ever dare to ask.

"When I am with Him, nothing frightens me," Brother Lawrence once wrote.

---

[175] St. John of the Cross, OCD, *The Ascent of Mount Carmel, The Collected Works of St. John of the Cross,* translated by Kieran Kavanaugh, OCD and Otilio Rodriquez, OCD (Washington, DC: ICS Publications, 1991) Book 2, Chapter 14, No. 2, page 192

In order to reach this state, we must take custody of our minds and orient ourselves to stay as close to God as possible, not just in prayer, but outside of prayer as well, careful not to do or say or think anything that might displease Him. In other words, we must become mindful of Him at all times with the eyes of our soul fixed upon Him, whether we're in prayer or involved in worldly activities.

"Since much time and effort are needed to perfect this practice, one should not be discouraged by failure," Brother Lawrence advises.

Instead, we must first ask for God's grace to develop this practice and then, confident of His aid, endeavor to practice it as faithfully as possible. "Check in" with Him as often as you remember, but always doing so "gently, humbly and lovingly, without giving way to anxiety or problems."[176]

The benefits far outweigh the demands of this practice.

First, faith becomes more intense and efficacious in all life's situations, especially in times of stress and temptation. "For the soul, accustomed to the practice of faith by this exercise, sees and senses God present by a simple remembrance. It calls out to him easily and effectively, thus obtaining what it needs."[177]

Second, this practice strengthens us and enables us to hope and trust in the God who is always there for us, no matter what the situation. We no longer feel alone when facing all of those seemingly insurmountable mountains of life but are instead aware of the One who dwells within us whose power surpasses all human understanding.

Third, this practice inflames the will with a sacred fire of love for God. "This soul thus inflamed can live only in the presence of God, a

---

[176] Ibid, Spiritual Maxim No. 28, pg. 43
[177] Ibid, Chapter 7, No. 33

presence that produces in its heart a holy ardor, a sacred zeal, and a strong desire to see this God loved, known, served and adored by all creatures."[178]

Fourth, this practice produces great intimacy with God, who is our constant Companion on the journey of life and who shares with us every moment of every day, from the menial to the momentous. It's a real relationship, and one that is entirely reciprocal.

It's easy to consider such a practice and think that it belongs only to the ranks of the cloister, but this is not true. It was meant for everyone, in all walks of life. Brother Lawrence was right in the thick of life, full of energy and vitality. Even in the kitchen, one could see that his spirit dwelled in God because he often did the work of two, yet never seemed harried. He gave each chore his attention, working neither slowly nor swiftly, dwelling in calmness of soul and an unalterable peace. So constant was the inner joy of his soul that he would often tell the Lord that he felt deceived because his Christian walk had thus far been so pleasant and not filled with the kind of suffering he expected.

The same can be true for us. Once we allow ourselves to come to a practical understanding of it — that God is really present within each of us at every moment of every day — feeling, thinking, hearing, seeing everything right along with us — and we become *aware* of this Presence within ourselves — a whole new dimension of life opens up. We suddenly become more conscious of living not only as a physical being, but as a spiritual being as well. Living with God in this way becomes the ultimate form of existence, the optimal lifestyle. Nothing can surpass it

---

[178] Ibid, No. 35

because His Presence is pure joy, even in the worst moments, the most severe trials, and it quickly becomes the greatest treasure of our life. In fact, we can become so intimately associated with Him that we no longer feel like ourselves without Him.

After plumbing such profound depths as these, we can clearly see that there is no comparison between the practice of the presence of God and the practice of mindfulness. Any attempt to equate them only makes the differences between the two all the more painfully obvious. Compared to the broad reach of the practice of the presence of God, mindfulness is nothing more than what it is — a sterile mental exercise that focuses on a single dimension of life — that which concerns only the self. There is no reciprocal awareness or loving or sharing with Another. It is empty of all but ourselves.

As Father Dubay attests, in all of his study of Buddhism, "I do not recall even once reading the word 'love' used in connection with their inner awareness."[179]

Some like to say that we can use mindfulness to teach ourselves how to focus on the presence of God within us but this statement defies logic. How can we teach ourselves to focus on God by teaching ourselves how to focus on ourselves?

And if it's just a matter of adapting a Buddhist technique to a Christian purpose, this once again begs the question — why bother if we have our own practices such as those described above? Do we really believe that a Buddhist technique can be any more effective than a

---

[179] Dubay, Father Thomas, S.M., *Prayer Primer: Igniting a Fire Within* (Cincinnati, OH: *Servant Books*, 2002) pg. 154

Christian practice empowered by God Himself?

It should be obvious by now that if one is living in the present moment in the presence of God, there is no need for mindfulness. The Christian practices not only replace it but thoroughly surpass it.

Where mindfulness offers a momentary escape from anxiety, the Christian alternative offers a *solution* to anxiety.

Instead of being aimed at a momentary improvement, the Christian version offers permanent transformation.

One is a quick fix, the other is a long-term opportunity for exponential personal growth toward the ultimate goal of our existence here on earth — union with God.

By the time we reach this summit of union with Him here on earth, we will have been freed from the source of all the misery and anxiety in our lives — sin. We will have been completely transformed into a totally new creation — not just an improvement of the old — but someone entirely new.[180] When we are united with our Creator, we will finally become who we were meant to be from the beginning of time. This is a grace that surpasses all understanding.

Needless to say, none of this will ever be acquired through Buddhist-centered mental practices, simply because their intent is self-enlightenment, not a loving union with God.

And for this reason, any attempt to integrate these practices will not only result in syncretism, but will fail to accomplish the aims of either practice.

The bottom line is that although *Nostra Aetate* allows us to

---

[180] Ephesians 4:24

acknowledge what is good in other religions, the Christian never *needs* to rely on other religions for spiritual growth. In fact, the purpose of our acknowledgement is to build a bridge in order to bring others into the fullness of the faith that we already possess! This is because we already have everything we need. Ours is a fully-functional faith. It's not just something we do for an hour on Sundays. It's something that we're meant to live, to integrate into our day-to-day lives, to experience alongside the One who dwells within us in each and every moment. Acquiring an awareness of not only the present moment, but of God's presence within that moment, becomes something truly life-changing because His presence impacts everything about our ourselves, our lives, and the world we live in.

Another Cup of Tea

As we conclude this guide, let us now return to the example of mindfulness from chapter one where we sat drinking a cup of morning tea, and recreate this scene in the Sacrament of the Present Moment and in the Presence of God.

As you may recall, in the mindfulness exercise, you were drinking a cup of tea and taking note of how it tastes, of the feel of the cup against your lips, the scent of the tea, the warmth of the liquid as it enters your mouth and courses down your throat, the thoughts that cross your mind as you swallow, etc. If you begin to think that perhaps the tea should be a bit sweeter or the noise of a truck on the road outside is a bit too loud, you simply return your thoughts to what *is* — a sip of tea that is a tad too bitter and a noisy truck passing by.

But in the Christian version, you are not drinking this cup of tea alone. You are sharing it with Someone who loves you beyond measure with a sure, unwavering, and ever-faithful love. An awareness of being in the hands of such an omnipotent and yet loving God inspires a profound security and contentment within you, as warm and gratifying as the tea that courses down your throat and splashes into your stomach. What is there to worry about when you are in the hands of Someone so powerful, Someone who is here in this moment as surely as He will be here in the next? What the day might bring doesn't matter. Right now, it's all about the tea, the quiet, the warmth, even the sudden disruptive sound of a noisy truck rattling down the road outside. It has all been willed for this moment, just for your benefit. And for this reason, it's all good, the pleasant and the annoying. Every time your mind tries to wander ahead into the day, your heart gently tugs you back to this moment as you sit at the kitchen table and drink a cup of tea with the One who holds your very life in His tender hands. You are content to sit with Him, for as long as this moment lasts, until the next one comes bearing another gift from Him, another revelation, another chance to love and be loved.

And so you are at peace, because you have found all that is worth seeking.

About the Author

Susan Brinkmann, O.C.D.S., author and award-winning journalist, is a member of the Third Order of Discalced Carmelites. She is the staff journalist for Women of Grace® and is a frequent guest on EWTN's *Women of Grace*® television show. She formerly wrote for *The Catholic Standard & Times,* the newspaper for the Archdiocese of Philadelphia.

In addition to two historical novels published by *HarperCollins,* she is the author of a book on Carmelite prayer, *Lord Teach Us to Pray,* published by *The Catholic Standard & Times.* Her book *The Kinsey Corruption* (published by Ascension Press) details the fraudulent research of Alfred C. Kinsey. Susan also published *The Learn to Discern Compendium: Is It Christian or New Age?* with Simon Peter Press. Liguori Publications published the story of her conversion, *We Need to Talk: God Speaks to a Modern Girl.* Her most recent publication, co-authored with Johnnette Benkovic, is *The Young Women of Grace Study Program* which teaches girls ages thirteen-plus about authentic femininity.

Her national journalism awards include the Bernadine-O'Connor Award for Pro-Life Journalism, the Eileen Egan Journalism Award from Catholic Relief Services, and numerous awards from the Catholic Press Association and the Philadelphia Press Association.

Made in the USA
Columbia, SC
08 June 2018